# UNMASKING AUSTERITY

## Opposition and Alternatives in Europe and North America

by
Dexter Whitfield

SPOKESMAN

Spokesman Books
Russell House
Bulwell Lane
Nottingham
NG6 0BT
www.spokesmanbooks.com

Published 2014
Paperback ISBN: 978 0 85124 8417
eBook ISBN: 978 0 85124 832 5

Acknowledgments

Many thanks to John Spoehr, Hugo Radice and Sol Picciotto and to Tony Simpson and Abi Rhodes of Spokesman Books

Three Briefing Papers on Unmasking Austerity, Opposing Austerity and Alternatives to Austerity by Dexter Whitfield were commissioned and published by the Australian Workplace Innovation and Social Research Centre and European Services Strategy Unit, with support from the Don Dunstan Foundation and the Public Service Association of South Australia, in August 2013 and February 2014.

www.adelaide.edu.au/wiseer

www.european-services-strategy.org.uk

## About the Author

Dexter Whitfield is Director of the European Services Strategy Unit and Adjunct Associate Professor, Australian Workplace Innovation and Social Research Centre, University of Adelaide.

He has carried out extensive research and policy analysis of regional/city economies and public sector provision, jobs and employment strategies, impact assessment and evaluation, marketisation and privatisation, public private partnerships, modernisation and public management (www.european-services-strategy.org.uk).

He has undertaken commissioned work for a wide range of public sector organisations, local authorities and agencies and worked extensively with trade unions at branch, regional and national levels in the UK and internationally. He has advised tenants and community organisations on housing, planning and regeneration policies.

Dexter is the author of In Place of Austerity: Reconstructing the economy, state and public services (2012); Global Auction of Public Assets: Public sector alternatives to the infrastructure market & Public Private Partnerships (2010); New Labour's Attack on Public Services: Modernisation by Marketisation (2006), Public Services or Corporate Welfare: The Future of the Nation State in the Global Economy (2001), The Welfare State: Privatisation, Deregulation & Commercialisation (1992) and Making it Public: Evidence and Action against Privatisation (1983). He was one of the founding members of Community Action Magazine (1972-1995) and Public Service Action (1983-1998). He has published articles in journals and delivered papers and advised public bodies and trade unions in Europe, US, Canada, Australia and New Zealand.

# Contents:

## List of tables



## List of figures

# Introduction

*Unmasking Austerity: Opposition and Alternatives in Europe and North America* exposes the failure and harmful effects of austerity and neoliberal policies. It shows how financial institutions, the International Monetary Fund, European Union, European Central Bank and governments imposed job losses and mass unemployment; wage, pension and welfare benefit cuts; and foreclosures and evictions on the poor and working class, who were forced to bear the brunt of the worst recession in over sixty years.

We now hear claims of 'growth' and 'recovery' by governments intent on maintaining austerity conditions for the foreseeable future. There is no commitment to restore what has been cut, closed or withdrawn.

Unmasking Austerity demonstrates how austerity policies have fuelled the fire of recession rather than stimulated growth. It examines austerity strategies in Europe and the US and assesses their economic and social effects. It explains why austerity failed and how the neoliberal reconfiguring of public services and the welfare state ran parallel to austerity policies.

Opposing Austerity identifies the key lessons from organising and action against austerity policies and challenges to the neoliberal transformation of public services and welfare states. It raises wider and longer-term issues about the way in which trade unions, community, civil society organisations and social movements mobilise and organise, widen support and build stronger alliances.

Alternatives to Austerity sets out an alternative to austerity through economic stimulus, reconstruction of public services and the welfare state, faster fundamental reform of banks and financial markets, the elimination of corporate welfare and strategies to increase the labour share of national income.

Exposing Causes, Contradictions and Conflicts discusses the deeper causes of the financial crisis and the manufactured crises being used to further dismantle hard-earned labour rights and the welfare state. It examines four of the contradictions and conflicts evident when campaigning for alternative policies to austerity and neoliberalism. The chapter concludes by calling for a radical rethink of trade union, community and social movement organising and action strategies.

Chapters 1-3 were originally published as separate briefings in Australia to widen understanding of the effects of austerity policies and the strategies needed to oppose to them. They have been updated together with the addition of the fourth chapter.

# Chapter 1
# Unmasking Austerity

## Key findings

Austerity was intended to rapidly reduce public debt by a combination of cutting public spending, reducing or freezing labour costs, tax increases and privatisation alongside reconfiguring public services and the welfare state. These measures would in turn allow the private sector to generate economic growth.

**Austerity has failed because:**

- Government debt has continued to increase.
- Reduced demand in economies has intensified the recession and the theory of 'growth friendly' fiscal consolidation has been discredited.
- Negative or weak economic growth has prevailed and the private sector has failed to fill the gap in investment created by significant reductions in public sector expenditure.
- With trading partners also in recession export led growth has been stunted.

**The economic and social effects of austerity:**

- Soaring economic costs – the loss of output, reduced wealth, unemployment and government intervention and support runs into trillions of dollars in the US alone.
- 5.5 million young people are unemployed in the European Union alone.
- 2.2m public sector job losses have followed deep cuts in public spending in the UK, US and Spain alone.
- Cuts in wages, benefits and pensions have reduced take-home earnings by up to 20%.
- Closures and business failures have increased in parallel with austerity.
- The financial crisis led to the bankruptcy of several US towns and cities.
- The house price slump resulted in large-scale foreclosures, mortgage arrears and between 10%-31% of mortgages in negative equity in the UK, US, Spain and Ireland in 2012-2013.
- Health services have suffered closures and patients face increased charges and longer waiting times.

- Austerity has increased poverty and widened inequality and public spending cuts increased inequalities between regions.

- Bailouts have protected bank bondholders, except in Iceland, in a gigantic wealth transfer from taxpayers to the corporate sector and wealthy individuals.

- Meanwhile corporate profits have risen, share price highs achieved in 2013 and cash hoarding by large US corporations has mushroomed.

- Public services and the welfare state are being reconfigured to embed marketisation and privatisation in parallel with austerity.

- Despite public spending cuts governments are widening corporate welfare through financial aid to the private sector, deregulating markets and increasing the role of business in public policy making.

- The idea that governments have no option but to adopt austerity policies is incorrect. Not only was the scale of austerity unnecessary, it was unjust and based on flawed economic theory.

## The switch from stimulus to austerity

Austerity was intended to rapidly reduce public debt by a combination of cutting public spending, reducing or freezing labour costs, tax increases and privatisation alongside reconfiguring public services and the welfare state. These measures would in turn allow the private sector to generate economic growth.

Systemic banking crises occurred in seventeen countries between 2007 and 2011, five of which were outside of the European Union and North America according to an IMF banking crisis database. Fifteen countries nationalised bank assets. A further eight countries, including Russia and Switzerland, were borderline – i.e. almost met the systemic criteria (Laeven and Valencia, 2012).

The bailout of banks and the collapse of revenue following housing and property crashes led to plummeting house prices and foreclosures in several countries. 'Bad banks' were established to manage the assets of failed banks by governments in the UK, Germany, Ireland, Spain and several other European countries.

Bailouts were needed in Ireland, Iceland, Portugal, Spain, Greece and Cyprus. Bailout terms and timetables were set by the troika of the International Monetary Fund (IMF), European Union and the European Central Bank.

The initial response to the crisis was essentially Keynesian with stimulus strategies, although many were considered inadequate. For example, almost 40% of the US$787bn (£474bn) American Recovery and Reinvestment Act programme was tax cuts that '... were probably only half or less as effective in stimulating demand as actual increases in government spending' (Krugman, 2013a).

However, the deficit hawks took control in 2010 when austerity policies became the core policy. In the run up to the G20 Toronto meeting the German government and the European Central Bank lobbied extensively for fiscal consolidation winning over the UK and Canada and leaving the US isolated (Blyth, 2013a). The G20 Declaration duly stated '..."growth friendly" fiscal consolidation plans in advanced countries and that will be implemented going forward' (G20, 2010).

## Cause of the financial crisis

There were three main causes of the financial crisis.

Firstly, it was caused by the failure of markets and deregulation. It was a private sector failure, not a sovereign debt crisis caused by excessive government spending. Deregulation in general and specifically the failure to regulate, monitor and review financial markets was a key factor. Unregulated markets are not efficient, stable or self-correcting. Neither do they produce socially and environmentally acceptable outcomes. The economic and financial models that focused on the threat of external shocks '... simply misled us – the majority of the really big shocks come from within the economy' (Stiglitz, 2013).

Secondly, financialisation and a private credit-led speculative boom ultimately led to the collapse of housing markets in the US, Spain, Ireland and Iceland. Securitisation, the slicing and dicing of packages of mortgages and other loans, created asset-backed securities for sale to other investors. Computer models predicted low risks, although the separation of credit decisions from debt management was inevitably high risk. It '... revealed an actual world of hyper-leveraged excessive lending, over-borrowing and willful risk blindness' (Blyth 2013a). The financial sector offered much higher profits than could be obtained through productive investment and led to the growing power of finance capital in the economy (Callinicos, 2012).

Thirdly, neoliberal ideology and values such as free trade, competition, debt-driven consumerism, tax cuts for the wealthy, deregulation and privatisation underpinned economic policies and attitudes. Democratic accountability and transparency were expendable whilst profiteering and exploitation were considered 'business as usual'.

The origins of the financial crisis lie in '... the intensification of the drive for shareholder value, which set high profitability thresholds for investment and exerted intense pressure on labour, delinking productivity and wage increases. With median wage growth depressed, and growing inequalities in wealth and incomes, the dynamic demand required by the shareholder-value agenda was provided by the expansion of credit, supported by low interest-rate policies; debt-based household spending allowed consumption to grow at a faster rate than incomes and wages' (Aglietta, 2012).

# Why austerity failed

## Government debt continued to increase

Public debt as a percentage of Gross Domestic Product (GDP) continued to increase in Spain, France, Ireland, Portugal, Italy and Greece between 2011-2013 (see Figure 1), the UK and US likewise, with a very small decline in Germany in the first quarter of 2013.

When pre-financial crisis debt ratios are taken into account, the increase is even more substantial. Ireland's debt to GDP ratio increased from 24.8% in 2007 to 125.1% in 2013; Portugal's increased from 62.0% in 2006 to 127.2% and Greece's rose from 106% in 2007 to 160.5% in 2013. The ratio rose in both the euro area (from 88.2% to 92.2%) and in the 27-country European Union from 83.3% to 85.9% (Eurostat, 2013a).

Public debt as a percentage of GDP increased in Australia between 2007-2012 from 14.6% to 32.4% but it remains the third lowest of the thirty-four Organisation for Economic Co-operation and Development countries (OECD, 2013a). Canada is in a similar position with 32.9% debt/GDP ratio but both federal and provincial governments have adopted austerity policies. *'Austerity has slowed the recovery instead of encouraging it'* (Canadian Center for Policy Alternatives, 2013). Ontario inflated debt projections that were '... *based on misleading assumptions and were deliberately intended to stoke an austerity agenda of service cuts and wage freezes'* (Hennessy and Stanford, 2013).

**Figure 1: Public debt as a percentage of GDP**

**Austerity policies have failed to stop debt from climbing in struggling euro-zone countries.**

Debt as a percentage of GDP for various euro-zone countries

1Q 2013:

Italy: 130.3%

Portugal: 127.2%

Ireland: 125.1%

France: 91.9%

Spain: 88.2%

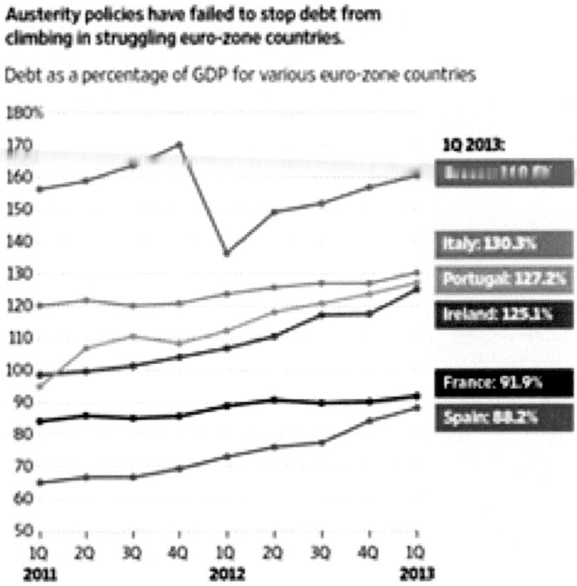

*Source: Eurostat and Wall Street Journal*

The frequently cited Reinhart-Rogoff paper (Growth in a Time of Debt) claimed that economies 'fall off a cliff when government debt exceeded 90% of GDP. Herndon et al

(2013) recalibrated the Reinhart-Rogoff model and concluded '... *average GDP growth at public debt/GDP ratios over 90 percent is not dramatically different than when debt/GDP ratios are lower'*. The '... *revelation that the supposed 90 percent threshold was an artifact of programming mistakes, data omissions, and peculiar statistical techniques suddenly made a remarkable number of prominent people look foolish'* (Krugman, 2013b).

## Less demand in the economy

Austerity increased unemployment, drove down wages, reduced and/or made welfare benefits more restrictive and cut government spending. In addition, households increased saving to pay off mortgage and consumer debt. Austerity agreements brokered by the IMF, EU and ECB included public spending cuts, tax increases, wage and pension cuts, public sector reform and privatisation. The scale of these measures was wide-ranging and draconian. Ireland's agreements in 2009 and 2011 were equivalent to 15.2% of take-home household income (all income, minus direct taxation and social insurance payments). The 2011 Greece austerity package alone represented 13.7% of take-home household income (Financial Times, 2011).

Advocates of 'expansionary austerity', such as Alessina and Ardagna, claimed that cutting public spending would lead to higher output, precisely the opposite of the Keynesian proposition that cutting spending in a weak economy would weaken the economy and trigger stagnation. Their work was influential in promoting the austerity strategy in the European Central Bank and other European institutions and has now been thoroughly discredited (Blyth, 2013b, Krugman, 2013a, 2013b, Quiggin, 2012).

> *Just as zombies are grim and distorted versions of their living selves, so the ideology of expansionary austerity is a grim and menacing version of the ideology of market liberalism (Quiggin, 2012).*

Forecasts for economic growth in the post-austerity period were systematically overstated by the IMF (and by the European Commission and the Organisation for Economic Cooperation and Development) (IMF, 2012a). The IMF originally claimed that 'fiscal consolidation', mainly public spending cuts, would have a relatively minor impact on economic growth. A fiscal multiplier of 0.5 was commonly used in austerity packages, but this did not fully take account of the economic and financial conditions in a recession. This 'justified' austerity measures, but dragged economies further into recession and stunted economic growth.

In this case, the selection of a low multiplier minimised the effect of austerity on economic growth. The same organisations have consistently overstated the economic and employment impacts of development and infrastructure projects and accepted at face value consultants exaggerated traffic and toll forecasts for PPPs.

The IMF's World Economic Outlook 2012 conceded that '... *the multipliers have actually been in the 0.9 to 1.7 range since the Great Recession' (IMF, 2012a)*. In other words, '... *the gap between reality and forecast is thus extremely large. The negative effects on economic growth have been three times as great as forecast by the IMF, EU or OECD'* (Hall, 2013).

> *Reducing public expenditures during a recession, in contrast, can be expected to increase the national debt as increasing unemployment and falling incomes lower tax revenues and increase social welfare payments (King et al, 2012).*

IMF researchers Blanchard and Leigh (2013) concluded that multipliers were significantly above 1 in the early years of the crisis. Auerbach and Gorodnichenko (2011) found fiscal multipliers of about 2.5 in a recession, and Batini et al (2012) revealed two-year cumulative multipliers of 2.49 for public spending cuts compared to 0.35 for tax increases in the Euro Area and 2.17 and 0.65 multipliers in the US.

> *... when account is taken of the magnified impact of consolidation in a depressed economy, and of the spillover effects of coordinated fiscal consolidation across almost all EU countries, fiscal multipliers will be considerably larger than in normal times, and the impact on growth correspondingly larger ... the policies pursued by EU countries over the recent past have had perverse and damaging effects (Holland and Portes, 2012).*

Public spending cuts accounted for 75% of austerity measures in the UK between 2010-11 and 2014-15. Public spending has declined sharply since 2008-2009 with further substantial cuts planned to 2018. Local government revenue spending reduced 12% in England between 2009 and 2013, but if schools, police and housing benefits are excluded (which are no longer in local authority control or which are demand-led), the reduction between 2008-2009 and 2015 rises to 29% in England and 24% in Scotland (Hastings et al, 2013). UK output per hour was 4.4% below the pre-crisis level by the end of 2013 and changed relatively little over the five-year period. The fall in labour productivity was more severe than economic crises in 1979 and 1990 when output per hour increased 12.6% and 19.9% by the same stage (Figure 2). It illustrates the scale of the deep recession in the UK and the weakest recovery on record (Office for National Statistics, 2014).

**Figure 2: Fall in UK labour productivity, output per hour (seasonally adjusted)**

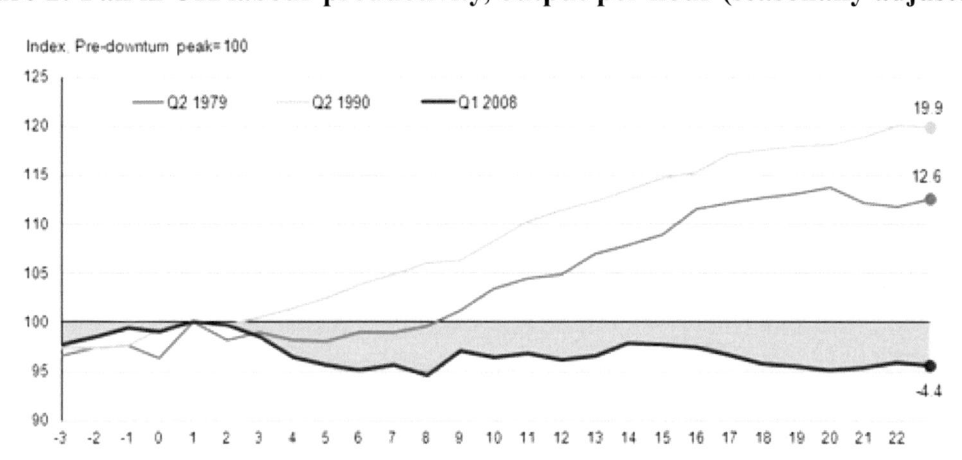


*Source: Office for National Statistics, 2014*

## Negative or weak growth

A stream of business closures and bankruptcies, bank restricted access to credit, reduced economic demand, coupled with drastic cuts in state and local government spending had a negative impact in regional and local economies. This led to a low level of business confidence and reluctance to invest.

The business investment rate fell to 19.7% in the Euro area and to 19.6% in the European Union 27 countries in the third quarter of 2012, significantly below the 2008 rate (see Figure 3) (Eurostat, 2013b).

**Figure 3: Investment rate of non-financial corporation in Europe (seasonally adjusted)**

*Source: Eurostat 2013*

Bank lending to non-financial corporations in the Euro Area plummeted in 2008-09, has a temporary recovery in 2011-12 only to fall again (see Figure 4).

**Figure 4: Bank lending to households andnon-financial corporations, Euro area**

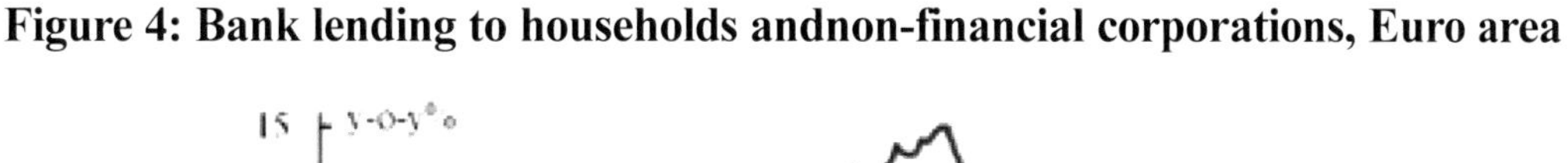

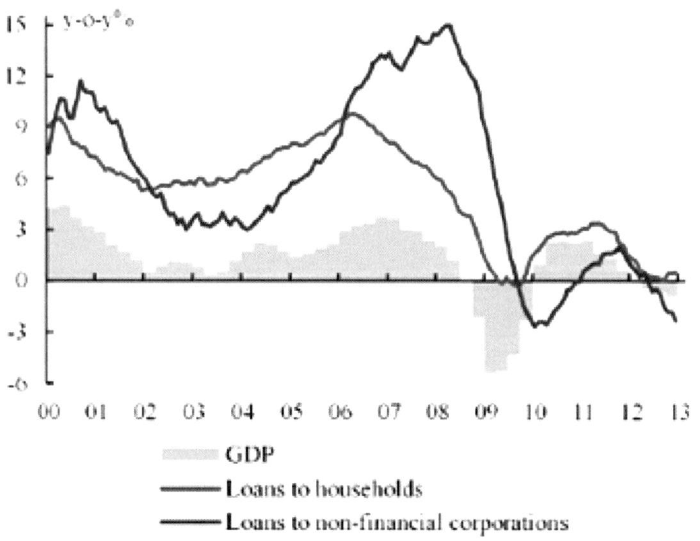


*Source: European Commission 2013a*

The Euro Area GDP growth rate since 2010 reached 1%, but has since hovered just above or below zero between last quarter 2011 and the first quarter 2013

Gross Domestic Product fell sharply in the Euro area, US and Japan in the financial crisis and was above zero after 2010 except the Euro Area reverted to negative in 2012 (see Figure 5).

**Figure 5: GDP growth rate Euro area, US and Japan 2000-2012 (annual % changes, quarterly data)**

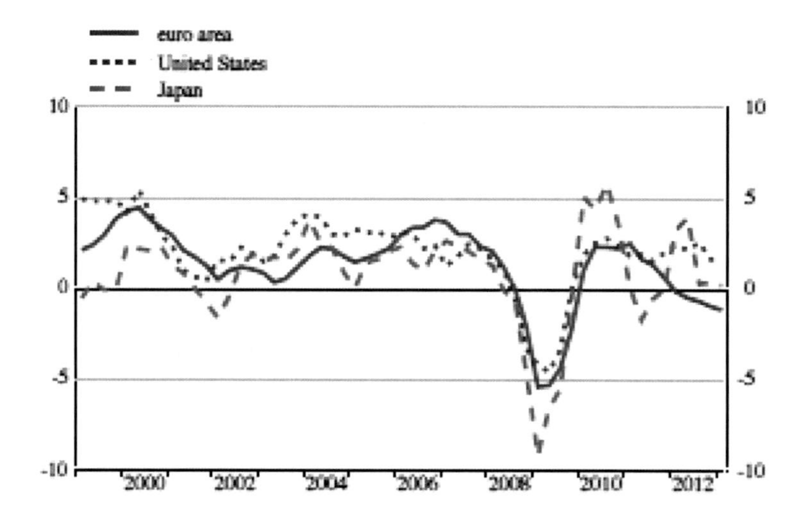


*Source: European Central Bank Monthly Bulletin, 07/2013*

Business start-up rates remain below pre-crisis levels, particularly in the Euro area according to July 2013 OECD data (see Figure 6). Australia and the UK show 'tentative signs of a pick-up in start-ups, but this is driven by sole-proprietor self-employed businesses.

Start-up rates are particularly low in Spain (OECD, 2013b). Business failures and bankruptcies are below the high rates reached in 2009-10, although rates in Denmark and the Netherlands increased in 2012 (ibid).

The IMF's analysis of the UK economy is for 'weak growth' and it is '*... still a long way from a strong and sustainable recovery. Notwithstanding the recent uptick in activity, per capita income remains 6 percent below its pre-crisis peak, making this the weakest recovery in recent history. Of particular concern is that capital investment (as a share of GDP) is at a postwar low, and that youth unemployment is high'* (IMF, 2013a).

Public spending cuts have reduced capital spending, particularly infrastructure investment, both direct investment and Public Private Partnerships (PPPs). Many countries have developed national infrastructure plans, but have lagged in project delivery. The global volume of project finance lending fell from US$159bn (£96bn) in 2011 to US$99bn (£60bn) in 2012 (Financial Times, 2013a).

**Figure 6: New enterprise creation 2007-2013**

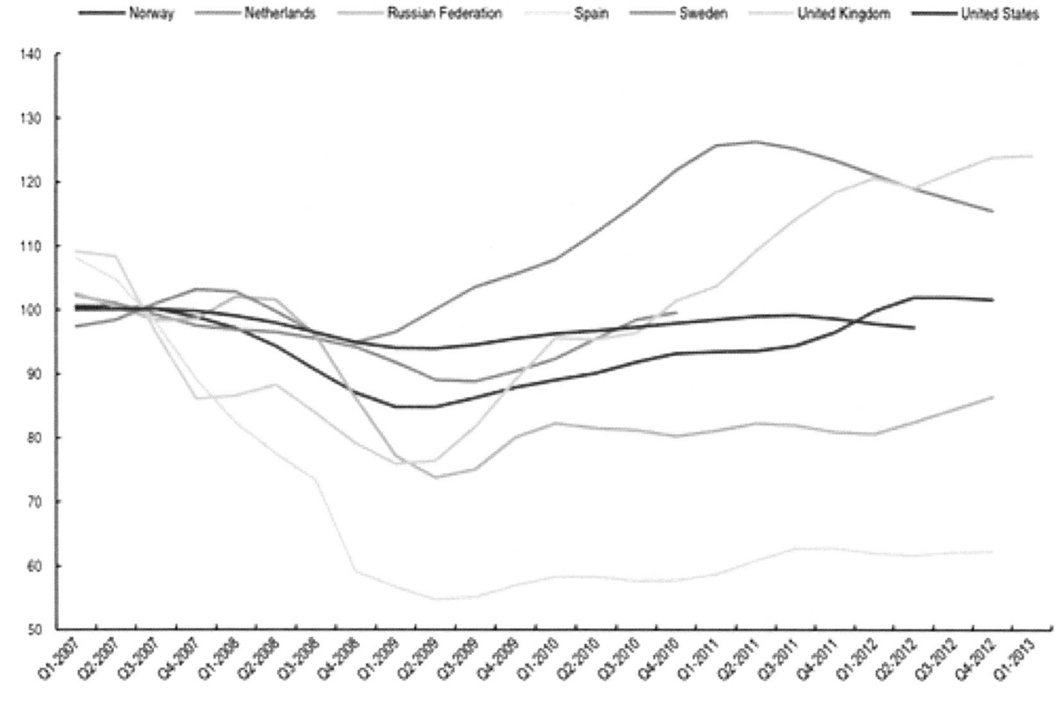

*Source: OECD 2013*

Although the financial crisis led to a slowdown in PPPs, particularly in the UK, austerity conditions led to an increase in governments approving PPP legislation and establishing central PPP units designed to ramp up the flow of contracts.

## Connected economies

Reduced economic growth in one country usually has a negative impact on growth in their trading partners, particularly if they too are also imposing austerity and seeking export-led growth. This is particularly the case in Europe where export-led strategies have been hampered by recession in the target countries. The Australian economy is affected by the economic performance of its main trading partners such as China, Japan and US.

Ireland, for example, has adopted an export-led growth strategy. A recent IMF Working Paper concluded the *'... decline in domestic costs registered since the crisis, together with the associated boost to inward FDI (foreign direct investment), suggests that even with the tepid external demand currently projected for the medium-term, Ireland can still register moderate exports growth and a boost to GDP and fiscal revenue'* (Nkusu, 2013). The study stressed that trading partners' demand is an important driver of exports and also the single most important driver of Ireland's GDP and revenue performance. It did not take account of *'... high household debt, high unemployment, and bank fragility'* and assumed that *'... public spending is kept in check'* (ibid). Ireland's exports are highly complicated by the presence of transnational pharmaceutical and IT companies and its low corporate tax regime.

A Central Bank of Ireland study reported *'... the vast majority of indigenous employment (which makes up 78 per cent of private sector employment) is still accounted for by traditional sectors such as Hotels & Restaurants, Wholesale & Retail, Business & Administrative services and Transport & Storage'* (Lawless et al, 2012). They stressed the importance of the domestic-demand driven services economy in job creation strategies.

## The economic and social effects of austerity

This is no short-term crisis. After five years of austerity policies every small sign of 'growth or 'recovery' has exaggerated significance. Yet most governments, particularly the bailout countries, Ireland, Portugal, Spain, Greece and Cyprus, plan further public spending cuts, labour market 'reform' and tax increases for at least the next five years. For example, unemployment in Spain is forecast to fall to 25.3% by 2018, only a marginal change from the current rate of 27.2% (IMF, 2013b).

### Soaring economic costs

The full cost of the financial crisis runs into trillions in any currency. It is important to distinguish between the overall cost of the financial crisis and the cost of individual bailouts in which the state may make a 'profit' at privatisation.

Lost output, measured as lost Gross Domestic Product (GDP), can range from 19% of pre-crisis GDP to 158% depending on whether the possibility of permanent effects are taken into account (Basel Committee on Banking Supervision, 2010).

Atkinson et al (2013) assess the US loss of output between US$6tn (£3.6tn) to US$14tn (£8.4tn) plus the cost of reduced wealth US$15-30tn (£9tn-£18tn), the cost of unemployment, lost opportunity and public trust of up to US$14tn (£8.4tn) and the cost of government intervention and support of US$12-13tn (£7.2-£7.8tn). US households lost about US$9.1tn in constant 2011 dollars (£5.5tn) in the value of home equity between 2005-2011 (Government Accountability Office, 2013a). The full social and human impact will probably never be known.

The fiscal costs of the financial crisis in the Euro Area and US between 2007 and 2011 were broadly comparable. The loss of output, increased debt, monetary expansion and fiscal costs were 55.1% and 67.0% respectively of GDP. However, the Euro Area had a significantly higher provision of liquidity support as a percentage of deposits and foreign liabilities (Laeven and Valencia, 2012).

The resale of shares, repayment of loans, fees from guarantees and other financial mechanisms may result in governments achieving a profit for individual programs, for example, the US Federal Reserve Bank gained US$17.7bn (£10.7bn) from loans to and asset purchases from the American Insurance Group. The net cost of the US Troubled Asset Relief Program has fallen to US$23bn (£13.9bn) compared to the US$419bn (£252bn) spent in bailing out companies since 2008.

The European Central Bank could eventually break even or make a surplus on the €276bn (£226bn) of assets it acquired between 2009 and 2012. Similarly the UK government must sell its stake holding in RBS and Lloyds banks for at least £34bn just to cover the total cash injected into the banks and the cost of financing the purchase of shares (National Audit Office, 2013). However, any gains are a drop in the ocean compared to the financial, economic and human cost of the crisis.

## Rising unemployment

Unemployment climbed to 26.9% and 26.8% in Spain and Greece respectively in May 2013 compared with the European average of 11%. Germany's rate was 5.3%, compared to the UK (7.7%) and US (7.6%). There were 5.5m young people (under 25) unemployed in the European Union. Youth unemployment continues to rise in the bailout countries led by Greece (59.2%), Spain (56.5%), Portugal (42.1%) and Ireland (26.3%) (see Figure 7) (Eurostat, 2013c).

**Figure 7: European youth unemployment**

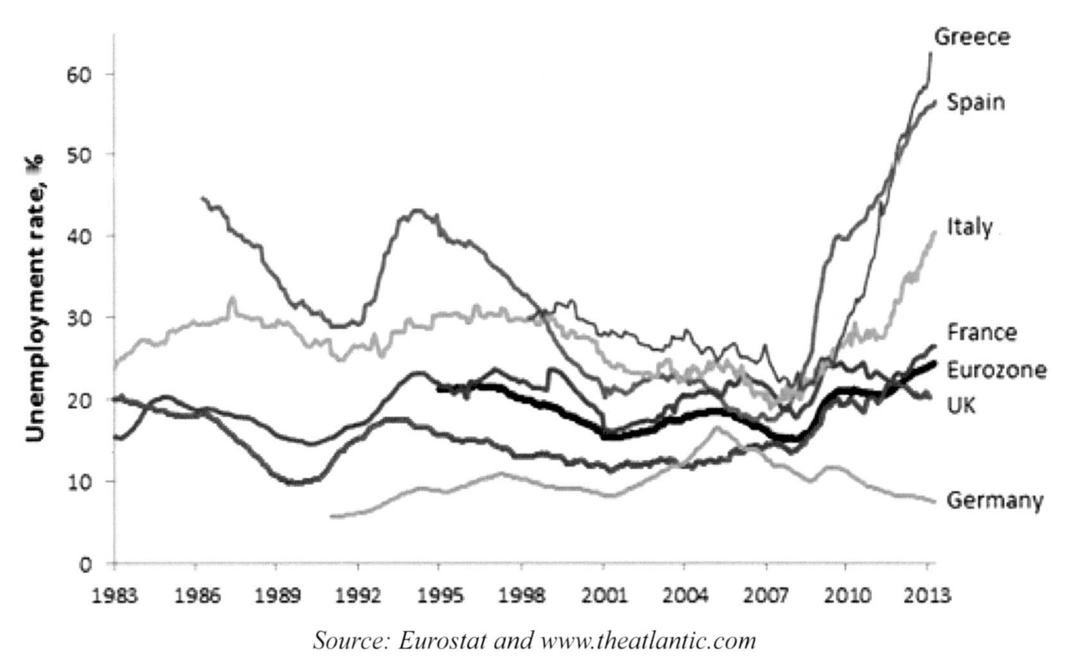


*Source: Eurostat and www.theatlantic.com*

The increase in unemployment in the younger age groups 16-17 and 18-24 in the UK between 2008 and 2013 is dramatically illustrated in Figure 8.

**Figure 8: Increased ILO unemployment rate by age in UK 2008-2013**

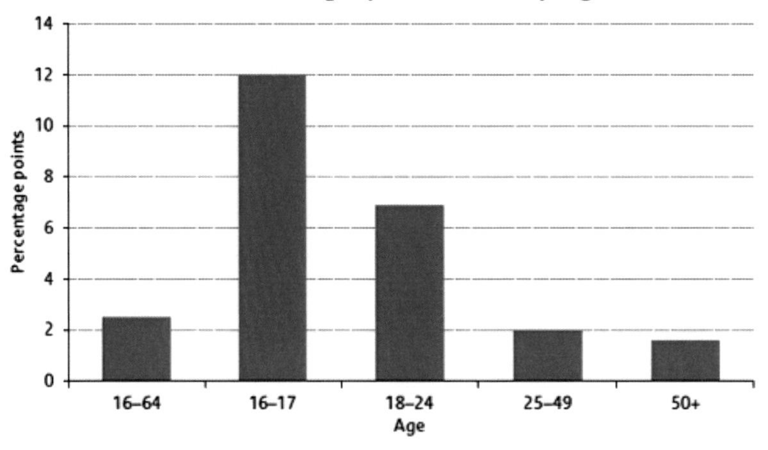


*Source: IFS Green Budget 2014*

## Public sector job losses

2.2m public sector jobs will be lost in just three countries: the UK (1.1m by 2018 – Office for Budget Responsibility, 2012), the US (737,000 between 2009-2013 – Economic Policy Institute, 2013a) and Spain (375,000 between 2011-2013 – Government of Spain, 2013). Nearly 45,000 public sector jobs were lost in Ireland between 2009 and the third quarter 2013 (see Figure 9). The public sector in Greece is required to lose 150,000 public sector jobs by 2015. Portugal plans to cut 15,000 by the end of 2014 and Canada will cut nearly 30,000 federal jobs. In addition, recruitment embargos, temporary and zero hour contracts have increased.

**Figure 9: Public sector job losses: Ireland**

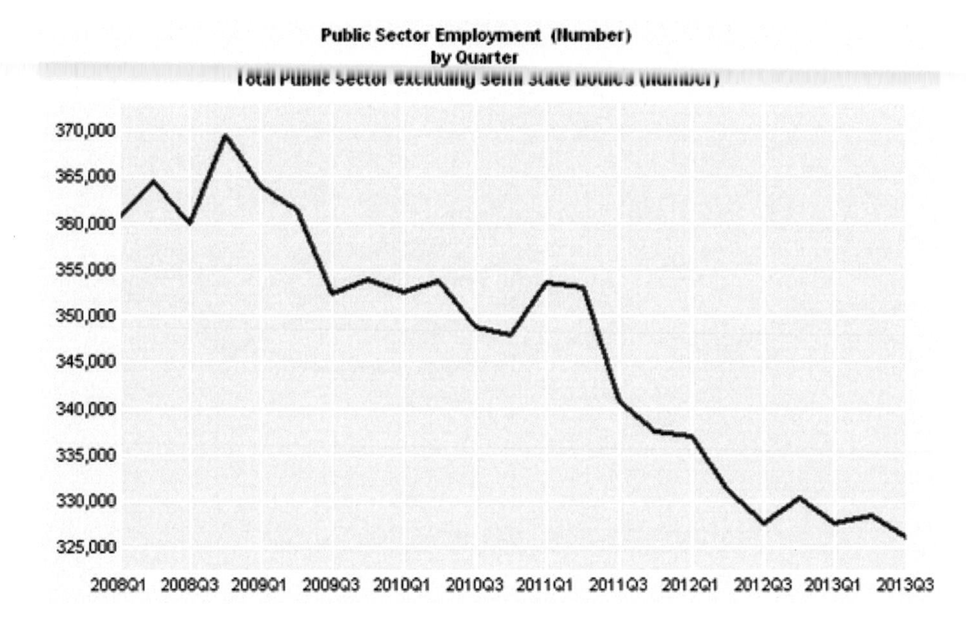


*Source: Central Statistical Office Ireland*

## Cuts in wages and benefits

Austerity policies have significantly reduced take-home earnings by between 5% and 20% in most European countries since 2008. They include pay cuts, reducing the starting pay of new workers, pay freezes, the withdrawal or reduction in allowances, bonuses and overtime payments (European Public Services Union, 2010).

Ireland imposed a pension levy equivalent to an average 7.5% of pay, changed pension arrangements for new starters from 2010 by raising the minimum retirement age from 65 to 66 and based pension payments on career average earnings rather than final salary (European Public Services Union, 2010). Other countries imposed similar measures.

The average funded ratio of US state pension funds fell from just over 80% in 2008 to 72.9% in 2011 as investment losses became evident in the actuarial value of assets. However, *'most states have sufficient assets in their pension trusts to fund payments over the near to medium term and in many cases, long term'* (Standard & Poor's, 2013).

Seventy seven per cent of the 598,000 net rise in new jobs in the UK since June 2010 are in low paid industries such as retail, catering and residential care with an average hourly wage of £7.95 – the 25 percentile of average hourly earnings (TUC, 2013). There is growing public and private use of zero hour contracts that provide no

**Figure 10: Growth of mini-jobs in Germany**

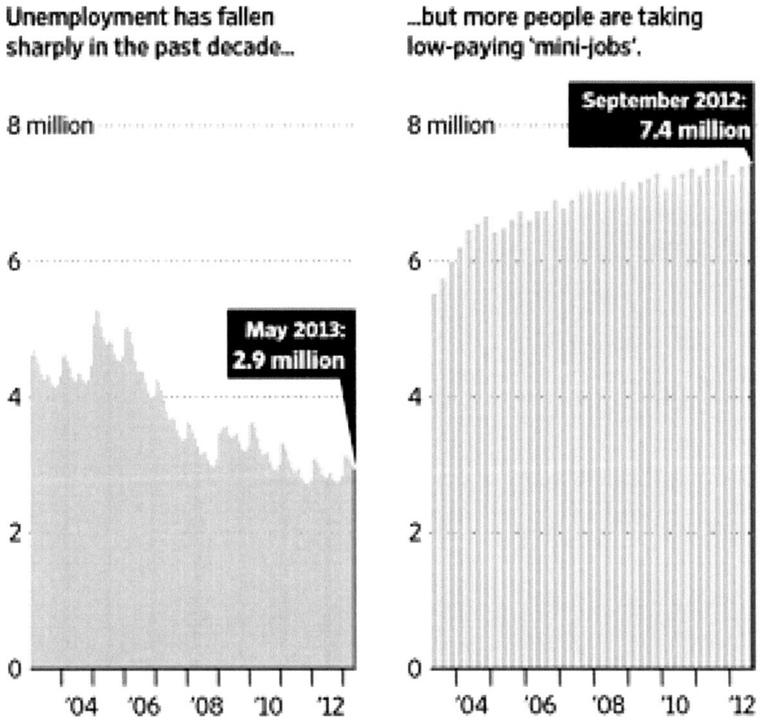

*Source: German Federal Employment Agency and Wall Street Journal*

guarantee of regular work and stability of income, sick pay or holidays. Austerity and marketisation of home care services has meant 97% of local authorities use homecare contracts that don't guarantee care providers any work from one week to the next. They in turn employ already low paid care workers on zero hour contracts, leading to worse services for the elderly (UNISON, 2013a).

Meanwhile, unemployment in Germany fell from 5m to 2.9m in the last decade. However, there has been a big increase in mini-jobs, which accounted for 7.4m workers or 20% of the workforce by September 2012. They are part-time jobs with low pay, flexible hours, hourly wages of between €5 (£4.10) and €10 (£8.20) per hour and workers can earn €450 (£369) per month free of tax. For two-thirds of mini-job workers it is their only job (Angelos and Adam, 2013).

The average annual UK public spending cuts per person have impacted four times more for those with a disability and nearly six times more for those in need of social care compared to the average cuts per person – see Figure 11. When the Welfare Reform Act 2012 has been fully implemented, together with earlier phased measures by the previous Labour government, they will take nearly £19bn a year out of the economy. The more deprived the local authority, the greater the financial hit (Beatty and Fothergill, 2013). Another study revealed that the government's welfare reforms will lead to *'... an astonishing £28.3bn being taken out of disabled people's pockets by 2018'* (Demos, 2013). It shows *'... how cuts to a host of benefits including Disability Living Allowance (DLA), Employment and Support Allowance (ESA), housing benefit and the 'bedroom tax' are hitting the same group of disabled people over and over again'* (ibid).

**Figure 11: Average annual UK cuts per person by 2015-2016**

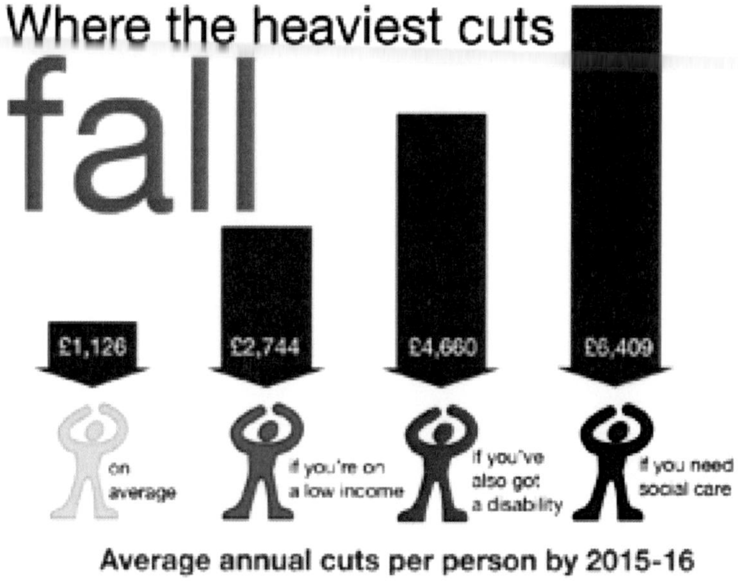

*Source: Duffy, 2013.*

## Closures and business failures

Corporate insolvencies in Western Europe (EU15 plus Switzerland and Norway) increased by a third between 2007 and 2011. Insolvencies continued to increase between 2010-2011 in the countries that had adopted austerity policies (Greece 27.3% increase, Spain 18.7%, Portugal 17.1%, Italy 16.9%, Ireland 7.0% and UK 6.3%) whereas they decreased in Sweden, Denmark, Germany, Austria and three other countries (Creditreform Economic Research, 2012).

UK retail business failures of medium and large companies soared to 54 in 2008, declined in 2010 only to increase again between 2011 and the first half of 2013. A second economic downturn led to weak retail sales and '*... the exiting of many companies that could survive a year or so of recession but not four years or low profits or losses. So far, 2013 looks to be even worse*' (Centre for Retail Research, 2013).

## Financial crisis of towns and cities

US ultra conservative political groups, think tanks and corporate interests have used austerity to impose more stringent fiscal discipline on states and cities (Peck, 2013). The American Legislative Exchange Council (ALEC) has widely promoted model privatisation legislation, tax cuts and drastic public spending and pension cuts.

Detroit filed for bankruptcy in 2013 with US$18.5bn (£11.1bn) debt and was preceded by Stockton, California (US$26m – £15.7bn) and Jefferson County, Alabama (US$4bn – £2.4bn) (Governing, 2013). Five other cities and towns had filed for bankruptcy since 2010, although three were dismissed. Another 28 utilities, water districts, hospital authorities and other municipal bodies had gone bankrupt in the same period. Counter to media claims, the crisis in Detroit and several other cities was not caused by costly pension schemes. Long argues that '*Detroit pays a relatively modest median pension*' and '*... well funded @ 82% in 2011 (and at 99% for its police and fire retirement system)*' (Long, 2013).

Bankruptcy and financial crisis has meant renegotiation of employment contracts, drastic cuts in services, reduction of pension fund obligations for current workers, outsourcing and sale of assets threatening the stability of the US$3.7tn (£2.2tn) municipal bond market. The City of Detroit's Plan of Adjustment submitted to the Federal Court in February 2014 requires the US$820m (£494m) sale of the Detroit Institute of Art to a new non-profit organization, funded by foundations, to cover pension obligations. Police and fire pensioners would receive 90% and other retirees 70% of what they are owed in pensions, but pensions would be frozen at their current level. Pensions could be re-negotiated after ten years if the pension schemes are financially healthy. Water and sewage and secured general obligation bondholders would receive 100% of their claim, but unlimited tax general obligation bondholders just 20% (Wall Street Journal, 2014a).

The longer-term financial squeeze on US cities led to wide use of Tax Increment Financing for development (future increases in the tax base are used to finance current investment), long-term leasing of existing infrastructure assets, such as toll roads and parking garages and meters, and economic development subsidies to retain or attract corporations.

European cities have traditionally relied on public/private borrowing and government transfers or grants than on bonds. UK local government spending cuts have forced the closure of libraries, children's centres, art and cultural facilities and restricted opening hours of others. The London Borough of Barnet is set to become the 'model neoliberal authority' through mass outsourcing (European Services Strategy Unit, 2012).

## Foreclosures and house price slump

The year-on-year changes in European house prices illustrate the dramatic falls in Ireland and Spain (see Table 1) (Standard & Poor's, 2013). Mortgage arrears continue to rise in Ireland – 12.3% (95,554) of residential mortgages were in arrears over 90 days at the end of March 2013. In addition, one in five mortgages for buy-to-let properties was in arrears over 90 days at the same date (Central Bank of Ireland, 2013). Irish mortgage arrears are expected to increase beyond the current 16.5% by value – about a third of distressed borrowers not in employment. The ratio of mortgage repayments to income is over 60% for a quarter of distressed borrowers, '... *so even debt write-downs may not be sufficient for a large cohort of borrowers'* (Davy Research, 2013).

**Table 1: Changes in European House Prices**

| European Nominal House Prices % Change Year On Year | | | | | | |
|---|---|---|---|---|---|---|
| | 2009 | 2010 | 2011 | 2012 | 2013 (f) | 2014(f) |
| Belgium | 1.1 | 5.8 | 2.0 | 1.4 | 0.5 | 1.5 |
| France | (4.2) | 7.7 | 3.7 | (1.9) | (4.0) | (4.0) |
| Germany | 1.5 | 2.9 | 6.8 | 3.6 | 3.0 | 3.0 |
| Ireland | (19.1) | (11.0) | (15.8) | (6.1) | (0.9) | 0.0 |
| Italy | (3.4) | (1.4) | (2.8) | (4.6) | (3.0) | (1.0) |
| Netherlands | (5.0) | (1.0) | (3.4) | (7.3) | (5.5) | (1.0) |
| Portugal | (0.6) | 1.6 | (0.9) | (2.7) | (3.5) | (0.5) |
| Spain | (6.6) | (3.3) | (7.1) | (10.5) | (8.0) | (5.0) |
| UK | 0.3 | 3.8 | (0.5) | 2.3 | 2.5 | 2.0 |

*Source: Standard & Poor's 2013 (f-forecast)*

The monthly rate of US home foreclosures soared to over 200,000 per month in 2009 (see Figure 12). There were 801,359 properties with default notices, scheduled auctions and bank repossessions in the first half of 2013, a 19% decrease on the previous six months. However, bank repossessions have risen in several states including Maryland, New York and Washington (RealtyTrac, 2013). In Ireland 31% of mortgages are in negative equity (Kennedy and McInhoe, 2012), 24% in Spain (Moody's, 2012), 21.5% in the US (PropertyWire, 2013) and 10% in the UK (Council of Mortgage Lenders, 2012). The UK figure masks wide regional variations with 35% in Northern Ireland and 14% in the North compared to 5% in the South East.

**Figure 12: US forclosures April 2005 to June 2013**

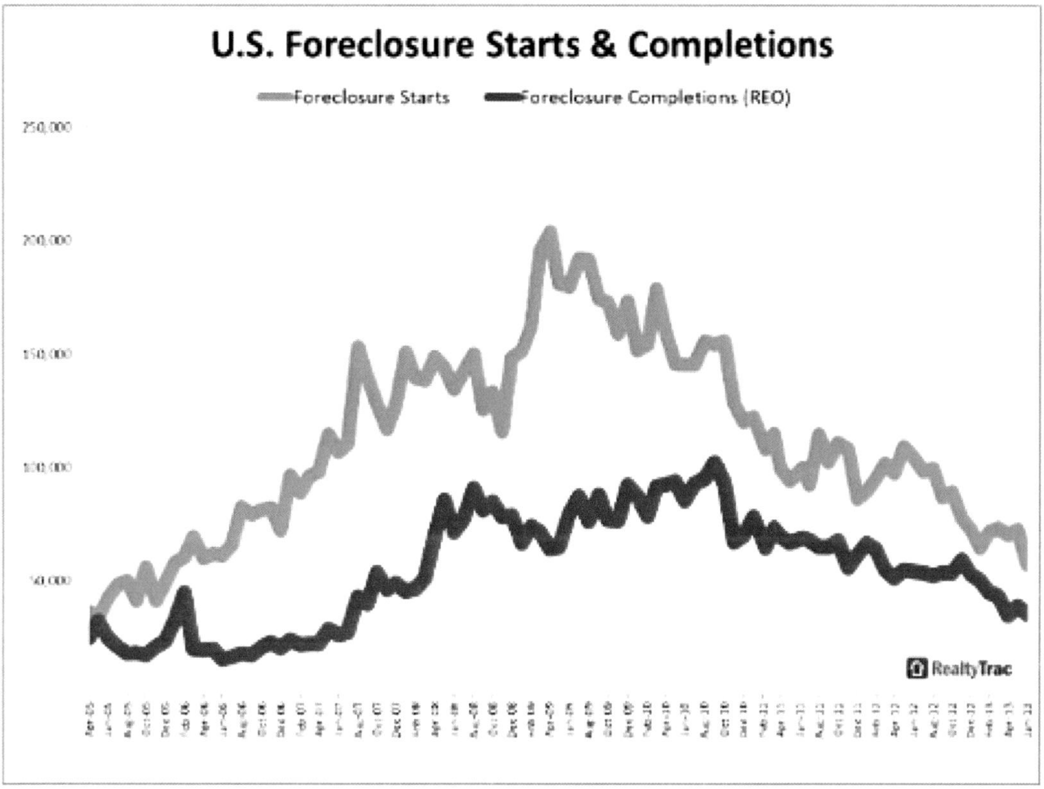

*Source: RealityTrac, 2013*

Household debt relative to disposable income soared in many countries up to 2008 and then declined. For example, the US household debt/income ratio declined from 130% in 2007 to 105% by the end of 2012, but household debt rose again in the second half of 2013 primarily due to a 12% increase in student debt to US$1.08tn (£650bn). *'The data reflect that many people going to college are in their 20s with less-established credit histories and thus lower scores. But the figures also could signal student debt is actually bringing down the credit scores of some borrowers as they fall behind on their payments and rack up high debt-to-income ratios'* (Wall Street Journal, 2014b).

Canada's household debt/income ratio reached an all time high of 163.4% in 2013 (Wall Street Journal, 2013c). Ireland's ratio declined marginally but remained a high 196.1% (Davy Select, 2014). UK household debt/income ratio increased to 170% in 2008, the declined to just over 140% in late 2013, but is forecast to rise again from 2014 (Resolution Foundation, 2013).

## Damage to health

Many European countries have reduced per capita spending on healthcare. Health systems have suffered closures, increases in a wide range of patient charges and longer waiting times (WHO, 2013). Spain shifted health coverage from a universal to employment based system in 2012 (Karanikolos et al, 2013).

Recession has led to increased suicide rates in Europe and the US (Stuckler and Basu, 2013). A long-term decline in infant mortality has reversed in Greece since 2008, with two consecutive years of increases. The number of stillbirths increased 32% since 2008 (WHO, 2013). A major upsurge in HIV infections among intravenous drug users coincided with a large reduction in funding for needle exchange programs.

Stuckler and Baus (2013) conclude not only did *'... the IMF underestimate austerity's economic harms, but it overlooked the even greater damage that resulted from cutting public health. Health and education had the largest fiscal multipliers, typically greater than 3.'*

## Poverty and widening inequality

Income from work and capital fell considerably in most OECD countries between 2007 and 2010, although welfare state benefits and lower income taxes (the automatic stabilisers) reduced the level of inequality. However, the richest 10% of the population did better than the poorest 10% in 21 countries (OECD, 2013c).

The OECD study covers the period up to 2010 before austerity measures began in earnest. If sluggish growth persists and fiscal consolidation measures are implemented, the ability of the tax-benefit system to alleviate the high (and potentially increasing) levels of inequality and poverty of income from work and capital might be challenged (ibid).

A UN Department of Social Affairs study examined fiscal consolidation measures for a sample of 17 OECD countries over the period 1978-2009. *'... fiscal consolidation episodes have typically led to a significant and long-lasting increase in inequality'* (Ball et al, 2013).

> *Across Europe the effect of the crisis on young people has been severe. While some of the overall effects have not been so great in the UK as in, say, Southern Europe, the way in which young adults have been disproportionately affected here has been similar. There is some irony that those who have been worst affected are those born in the decade – the 1980s – when financial liberalisation was set in train, ultimately contributing the financial crash that precipitated the crisis (Hills et al, 2013).*

Public spending cuts have often increased inequalities between regions. An analysis of local authority expenditure in England revealed London and the South East gained a net £235m between 2010 and 2012, but other regions had a net £4.5bn cut in resources. Of the top 50 most deprived local authorities, 46 suffered a reduction in funding that was above the English average (Special Interest Group of Municipal Authorities, 2013). This makes a mockery of the claim that 'we are all in it together'.

The economic impact on families is worsening:

> *A two-child family, with parents working as a nurse and on an average private sector worker's wage, will lose 18.9% or £8,009 by 2015. The lowest paid workers have faced the hardest hit; a single healthcare assistant with income when adjusted for tax and benefit top ups, the pay freeze, service cuts and inflation (UNISON, 2013b).*

Austerity has increased inequalities and restricted rights and non-discrimination across the board with the loss of jobs and cuts to wages, benefits and pensions; reduced access to employment; widened the gender pay gap; cuts in welfare state benefits and allowances; increased taxes and charges for public services including cuts in personal budgets; the closure of local facilities and services; decreased public funding of non-governmental and community organisations; the weakening of equality laws and draconian budget cuts in some equality authorities.

Black, Asian and Minority Ethnic women are more likely to be employed in the UK public sector than white women or men in the same ethnic group and suffer the impact of public sector job cuts. Unemployment among Black, Asian and Minority Ethnic women in Coventry increased 74.4% between 2009-2013, whereas it increased by 30.5% for white British women in the same period (Sandhu, 2013).

## Bank bondholders protected except in Iceland

Demands for bank bondholders to be 'burned' or take a 'haircut' (suffer losses) have been prominent in the media. Governments, banks and corporations sell bonds to finance long-term investment with a contractual agreement to repay the capital at a fixed date and make regular interest payments and can often be resold in the secondary market. For example, Anglo-Irish Bank's eighty bondholders in 2010 were a cross section of German, French, UK and other banks and financial institutions including Deutsche Bank, Goldman Sachs, HSBC, Credit Suisse and Barclays holding over €4bn (£3.3bn) of Anglo bonds.

Depositors (the public and businesses) together with tax authorities and senior debt holders have priority if a bank has a financial crisis, followed by bondholders, owners of asset-backed securities and shareholders (wealthy individuals and financial institutions). Depositors and bondholders were protected in earlier bailouts, but not in the €23bn (£18.8bn) bailout to recapitalise banks in Cyprus. The Laiki Bank will be wound down with EU insured deposits of €100,000 (£82,000) or less moved to the Bank of Cyprus. Uninsured investments in Laiki Bank over this limit, many held by offshore investors including wealthy Russians, will have 47.5% of their deposits converted into shares with the money used to contribute €4.2bn (£3.4bn) to the bailout. In this case the ECB and EU found it politically expedient to demand a 'haircut' or 'bail-in' of investors, whereas they have previously protected investors, fearful of the response of financial markets increasing borrowing costs and ratings agency downgrades.

Investor protection has been at an enormous cost as the following illustrates;

> *... a €200 billion subsidy to sovereign creditors is a gigantic wealth transfer from the taxpayer to essentially the richest 5% of the world. In the US, the 5% richest households control roughly 70% of all financial wealth, and this percentage is not much different in the rest of the world. Ultimate ownership of bank capital and sovereign debt is so concentrated among high-wealth individuals that we should characterise the bailout subsidy as ... a wealth tax supporting the rich* (Hau, 2011).

This is another example of the socialisation of losses and privatisation of profits.

Iceland privatised its banking system in 2000 which rapidly expanded into international markets. Three years later house finance was deregulated resulting in a house price boom. Iceland, not an EU member, raised interest rates up to 15%. Funds flowed in and bank loans and assets were more than ten times the country's GDP. The financial crisis in 2008 led to a sharp depreciation of the krona and the three largest banks became unsustainable. The government let the banks go bankrupt, devalued the krona, imposed capital controls and secured a US$10bn (£6bn) loan from the IMF and other countries. Three new banks were set up to take over the domestic assets of the collapsed banks. Although it was a costly recapitalisation it was significantly less costly than Ireland's bailout.

The Icelandic crisis led to across the board wage cuts, tax increases, public spending cuts, lost savings and 25% of homeowners in mortgage default. Large demonstrations led to voters twice rejecting repayment agreements for foreign investors (Mosesdottir, 2013). GDP expanded 4.6% in the first quarter of 2013 over the previous quarter and *'... competitiveness gains have been sustained, should help attract investment and support the recovery. We project growth of around 2 percent a year over the next five years'* (IMF, 2013c).

## Meanwhile corporate profits rise, share price highs and cash hoarding

As the consequences of austerity policies and continuing recession bite, it is business as usual for much of global capital. Profits have rebounded, particularly in financial companies such as Goldman Sachs, JPMorgan Chase, Citigroup, who were at the centre of the financial crisis. The US Dow Jones Industrial Average, the Standard & Poor's 500 and Nasdaq Composite recorded all-time highs in July 2013. US corporate profits soared to 12.4% of GDP in 2012, the highest level since 1943 (see Figure 13).

**Figure 13: US corporation profit as a percentage of GDP**

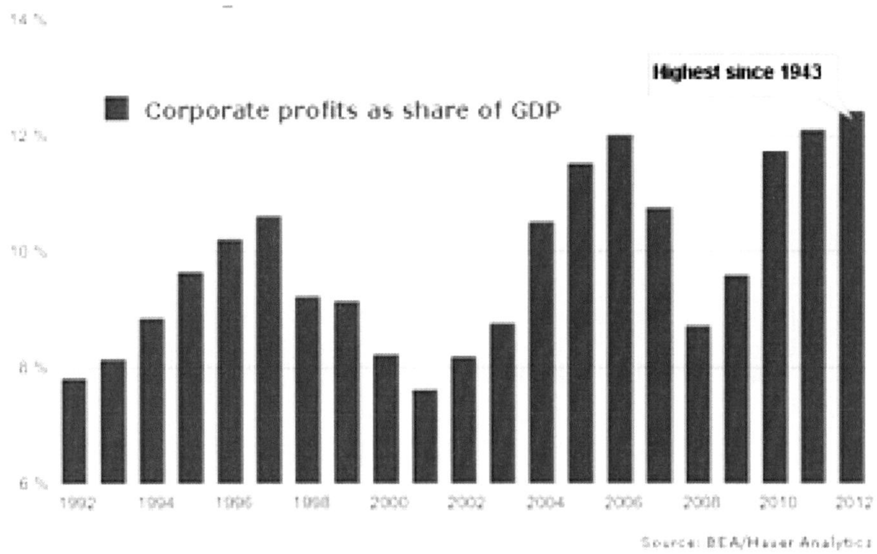

*Source: Wall Street Journal, 2013b*

The cash hoard of the one thousand largest US non-financial companies rose to US$1.5 trillion in 2013, an 81% increase since 2006, primarily an attempt to avoid US taxes (see Figure 14) (Moody's Investor Services, 2013).

> *American companies reported earning 43% of overseas profits in Bermuda, Ireland, Luxembourg, the Netherlands, and Switzerland in 2008, while hiring 4% of their foreign workforce and making 7% of their foreign investments in those economies* (Congressional Research Service, 2013).

**Figure 14: Cash hording by HS non-financial companies 2006-2013**

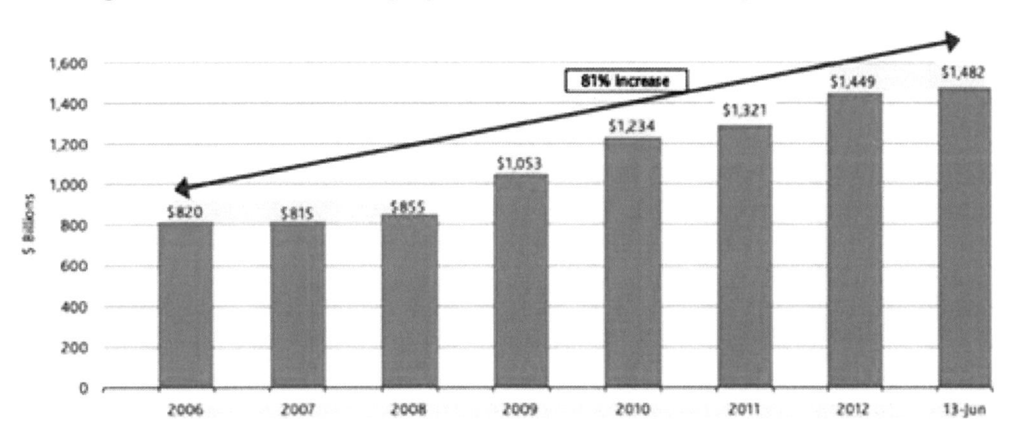


*Source: Moody's Investor Services*

Sixty US companies parked US$166 billion overseas in 2012. Many technology and healthcare companies have transferred intellectual property, such as patents and marketing rights, to subsidiaries in low tax countries (Wall Street Journal 2013c).

Lost revenue is even more critical when governments are trying to reduce debt and fund stimulus projects. However, tax avoidance is escalating as corporations exploit differences in the tax treatment of debt and equity, tax competition between countries and gaps in tax treaties and the rise of 'stateless income'. Corporate tax accounted for 22% of Australia's federal tax receipts in 2011-12, a higher share of GDP than most other OECD countries, but it is confronted by the same risks as other countries (Australian Government Treasury, 2013).

## Reconfiguring public services and the welfare state

The political, financial and business interests that believed austerity was the 'only option' were equally committed to embedding neoliberalism in the public sector and welfare state and reconfiguring the role of the state. Reconfiguration centred on marketisation and privatisation, with a new emphasis on financialising and personalising services to create new pathways to privatisation. The mutation of privatisation recognised that public services could not be sold off in the same way as state owned corporations (Whitfield, 2012a and 2012b). In fact, financialising and personalising services were essential to reconfigure public services to ensure that marketisation and privatisation were permanent and not dependent on outsourcing, which could be reversed by terminating or not renewing contracts.

Austerity did not create a 'new opportunity' to reconfigure the state, nor was it an example of 'shock doctrine'. The financial crisis merely allowed the acceleration of reconfiguration, because the implementation of neoliberal policies in the public sector and welfare state has been systematic and continuous for over three decades. The financial crisis, austerity policies and subsequent recession created new opportunities to advance private ownership, finance and service delivery; freedom of choice through competition and markets; deregulation; the deconstruction of democracy to increase the role of business in public policy making and to consolidate corporate welfare; and reduce the cost and power of labour.

There is a real danger that the 'automatic stabilisers' of unemployment and welfare state benefits will not be so effective in the next recession, because they may be privatised with more restrictive access and be less beneficial financially.

Public expenditure cuts and subsequent severe budget constraints have increased pressure to outsource, although much of UK local government regards this as a policy of 'last resort'. The promotion of social enterprises and voluntary sector contracting and the parallel promotion of a social investment market and social bonds, have aided this process. The closure of libraries, children's centres and other local facilities with many others reduced to statutory minimum, has made a mockery of 'localism'.

The fracturing of the state has been extensive. Academies, free schools and US charter schools, have opted out of local government to become part of private profit and non-profit chains. Other services have been transferred to trusts and social enterprises or to arms length trading companies. New business dominated Local Enterprise Partnerships are now responsible for economic planning and investment in the UK with large sums of redirected public money.

The merger of austerity and neoliberal policies is illustrated by the Organisation for Economic Co-operation and Development's attitude to 'structural reform of the labour market'. Reducing the cost of labour, 'improving the responsiveness of wages to labour market conditions' and market liberalisation have been implemented in Greece, Ireland, Italy, Portugal and Spain (Organisation for Economic Co-operation and Development, 2013d). The OECD has long promoted privatisation and neoliberal public management.

It regards 'successful' labour market reform to include reducing notice periods for dismissal, reducing severance pay, 'easing the difficulty of dismissal and procedural inconvenience', decentralizing and weakening collective bargaining, cutting unemployment benefit rates and shortening their duration. *'One sign of progress is the declines that have occurred in the OECD indicator of employment protection legislation in many of these countries'* (ibid).

Austerity and five key neoliberal objectives have legitimated new ways to financialise and personalise public services as a precursor to marketisation and privatisation (see Table 2). These policies are designed to destabilise and disinvest in public services and to dispossess, depoliticise and disempower service users, community organisations, staff and trade unions.

In sum, marketisation and privatisation provide new opportunities for accumulation, to gain more power and control in the economy, transfer risk, cost and responsibility to individuals and enable capital to radically reduce the role of the state, yet safeguard

**Table 2: Embedding neoliberalism in public services and the welfare state**

| Neoliberal objectives | Neoliberal pathways in public services and welfare state | Consequences of neoliberal policies |
|---|---|---|
| Free trade, competition & markets to allocate resources and deliver services | Financialisation | Destabilise |
| Deregulate to create new opportunities for accumulation | ↓ Personalisation | Dispossess |
| Deconstruct democracy to partnership with finance & business and consolidate corporate welfare | ↓ Marketisation | Depoliticise |
| Reconfigure the role of the state | ↓ | Disinvest |
| Reduce the cost and power of labour | Privatisation | Disempower |

corporate welfare. *'... we are witnessing a consolidation and centralisation of class power into the hands of a few institutions that escape public control'* (Harvey, 2010).

## Embedding corporate welfare

Political, financial and business interests are equally committed to ensuring the continuation and enhancement of corporate welfare. This has three elements:

Firstly, direct financial aid in the form of grants, subsidies, tax breaks and guarantees.

Secondly, market-making and outsourcing lead to a shared client/contractor ideology, values and vested interests in which the state outsources an increasing range of services, functions and infrastructure provision. Support for markets extends from the creation of, and support for, local economies to international Free Trade Agreements.

Thirdly, regulatory concessions to reduce 'red tape' and the cost of doing business, for example, curtaining the scope and penalties in health and safety and employment regulations.

Corporate welfare requires the state to adopt a business-led partnership model of governance for a wider range of functions, for example, Local Enterprise Partnerships for economic development and investment and Public Private Partnerships for infrastructure projects. Deep public spending cuts and welfare state restructuring imposed new or increased charges for services, restricted access to welfare benefits, initiated a blame culture that led to attacks on immigrants, which further atomised the poor and working class.

The focus on economic and financial matters led to democratic governance and accountability, equalities and environmental sustainability being marginalised.

## Lessons learnt

The idea that governments have no option but to adopt austerity policies is incorrect. Not only was the scale of austerity *'... unnecessary and ill-timed'* (Wolf, 2013), it was unjust and based on flawed economic theory. Furthermore, austerity *'... is a dangerous idea, because it ignores the externalities it generates, the impact of one person's choices on another's, and the low probability that people will actually behave in the way that the theory requires'* (Blyth, 2013b).

An alternative strategy should set out policies to reconstruct the economy, the state and public services. Economic and industrial policies should target investment for a clean-energy economy, infrastructure investment, job creation and the reform of financial institutions and regulatory regimes.

The socialisation of losses and privatisation of profits is the prime political and economic objective of austerity. Working people and the poor are made to pay for the failure of the banks, financial markets and wealthy elites.

Austerity has both short and long-term consequences that extend well beyond the implementation of the policy, for example, the loss of output, lost or delayed investment, health inequalities and poverty, the social effects of unemployment, migration and the loss of skills will be borne for years.

Comprehensive regulation, monitoring and review is a fundamental part of all sectors in the economy to ensure objectives are achieved. They must be democratically accountable and transparent and should not be drawn by corporate interests alone, nor left for them to self-monitor. The financial cost to the state and private sector should be accepted as a basic cost of public service or business.

Public spending cuts led trade unions and community organisations to launch anti-cuts campaigns. However, the focus on spending cuts diverted attention from the equally damaging imposition of neoliberal policies in public services and the welfare state. Alternatives to austerity and action strategies should therefore challenge neoliberal ideology and values.

## Recovery?

Some economies have technically come out of recession and Spain and Ireland have exited their bailout programmes, but this has had little effect on jobs and living standards. Indicators of economic growth and increased employment are small, anaemic and volatile in most countries. Emphasis on numbers belies the real quality of jobs being created.

Growth has slowed in the emerging economies – the BRICs (Brazil, Russia, India, China and South Africa) – and currency/investment problems have emerged in others.

The IMF's Global Prospects and Policy Challenges report for the G20 Finance Ministers February 2014 meeting in Sydney, Australia concluded *'... the recovery is still weak and significant downside risks remain. Capital outflows, higher interest rates, and sharp currency depreciation in emerging economies remain a key concern and a persistent tightening of financial conditions could undercut investment and growth in some countries given corporate vulnerabilities. A new risk stems from very low inflation in the euro area, where long-term inflation expectations might drift down, raising deflation risks in the event of a serious adverse shock to activity'* (IMF, 2014).

The IMF recommended that fiscal consolidation *'... should continue at a gradual pace'* and support the long-run growth potential of economies by enhancing infrastructure investment (including PPPs) and to broaden the tax base (ibid).

The reform of banks and financial markets is unfinished and questions remain about the effectiveness and sustainability of the reforms being implemented. The big banks are bigger, the shadow banking system is widening, the rich are richer and the system depends more than ever on investor faith in central banks (Tett, 2013).

Furthermore, the days of financial innovation, exotic mortgage products and complex swap deals are unlikely to be over. New derivatives or financial contracts may be developed in project finance as an increasing share of public infrastructure is financed by Public Private Partnerships (PPPs). A return on equity of 12%-15% is usually built into PPP contracts. However, an average 29% return was obtained in the sale of equity in 226 PPP projects in 93 transactions in the UK between 1998-2012 (Whitfield, 2012c). A combination of high rates of return, a growing global market, the increasing sale of concessions of existing infrastructure assets and new PPP models combining infrastructure and core service provision could generate a new phase of financial innovation including interest rate, currency, credit and equity swaps. Furthermore, the social investment market and social impact bonds are in their infancy and are likely to attract new financial 'products.'

Finally, we must remember the crisis was caused by the failure of markets and deregulation. It was a private sector failure, not a sovereign debt crisis.

Austerity has meant deep public spending cuts, mass unemployment, closures, privatisation, wage and benefit cuts, increased poverty and damage to health. Poor and working/middle class families have borne the brunt of the economic and financial burden of austerity – the socialisation of the losses. Income and health inequalities have widened.

Two UK coalition government policies demonstrate the class divide and ideology of austerity.

In 2012 the Coalition introduced a 'bedroom tax' on housing benefit claimants who face a 14% cut in their benefit if they are deemed to have a 'spare' bedroom. It penalises separated parents who share the care of their children, parents whose children visit, but are not part of the household, couples who use their 'spare' bedroom when recovering from an illness or operation and disabled people including people living in adapted or specially designed properties. The tax led to widespread opposition by tenants, trade unions and local authorities. Some authorities are re-designating bedrooms and refusing to evict tenants in arrears because of the 'bedroom tax'.

The Coalition government then imposed a cap on welfare spending for a four-year period from in 2015-16. It will have a 2% margin to allow small fluctuations '… but will not allow for discretionary policy action which breaches the level of the cap' (HM Treasury, 2014). State pensions and unemployment benefit are excluded, but includes an array of other important benefits for disabled people, single parents, carers and the low paid. 'Treasury forecasts show the bulk of the government's deficit reduction plans are to avoid tax rises in favour of attacks on social security spending. Ministers expect to impose £2bn of tax rises in 2015-16 compared to £21bn of welfare savings' (Inman, 2014).

The evidence demonstrates that austerity and neoliberalism have led to:

- A destabilised weaker economy;
- Dispossession of wages, pensions, homes and services;
- Depoliticisation as management of the economy is increasingly ceded to business interests and technocrats;
- Disinvestment in the public infrastructure and economic development;
- Disempowerment of trade unions, community and civil society organisations.

But there are organizing and action strategies and alternative policies that provide a way forward and the path to a more equitable and sustainable economy.

# Chapter 2
# Opposing Austerity: Organising and Action Strategies

## Key Findings

Action strategies deployed in the struggle against austerity and neoliberal policies provide lessons for how strategies might be developed in other countries. They raise wider and longer-term issues about the way in which trade unions, community and civil society organisations and social movements mobilise and organise, widen support and build stronger alliances.

- Although the financial crisis was caused by banks and market failure, action was targeted against government and troika-imposed public spending and wage/pension cuts, job losses and privatisation.

- Despite the worst economic crisis for 60 years, Labour and Democratic parties failed to deliver significant alternative policies or legislative change.

- The attack on public sector unions, workers' rights and legislation to reduce the ability to take industrial, civil and community action, ran parallel with public sector cuts and privatisation.

- Traditional industrial action, such as one-day strikes and large national demonstrations had an important role in strengthening solidarity and gaining support, but did not significantly change austerity policies.

- Cuts campaigns had an important role in challenging the composition and distributional impact of austerity policies, but rarely reduced the scope or scale of public spending cuts.

- A series of large public demonstrations at the Iceland Parliament, culminated in the resignation of the government and two referenda voting against taxpayers funding repayment of bank debt.

- The Quebec student strike stopped tuition fee increases, UK hospital campaigns stopped closures, many foreclosures and evictions were halted in Spain and US – all had active engagement of trade unions, community and social movements and drew wide public support.

- Democratic assemblies genuinely involved participants in discussion and decision-making in Spain's 15M and the Occupy Wall Street movements.

- UK trade unions have not developed adequate strategies to challenge the acceleration of neoliberal transformation of public services through outsourcing, private finance and privatisation.

- New national and local organisations and alliances created to resist foreclosures and evictions used imaginative direct action tactics, particularly in Spain and US.

- Trade unions are the strongest working class membership and resourced organisations. There are different types of membership organisations, such as student unions, worker centres and community organisations, plus involvement or affiliation to social movements. They must forge and sustain stronger alliances and coalitions.

- The process of learning lessons and developing future strategies needs to take account of the shifts in power, which the financial crisis and austerity measures have brought about.

- Divisions between pro- and anti-outsourcing strategies in the UK voluntary sector, mirroring a similar division in US non-profits, stunt the sector's opposition to austerity policies.

- Transnational Free Trade Agreements are being negotiated that will continue austerity measures, embed neoliberal policies and increase corporate power.

- Austerity measures will continue for many more years; cuts to services, jobs and wages will not automatically be 'restored', and government's will seek to consolidate economic 'reforms' alongside the 'transformation' of public services and the welfare state.

## Challenges in opposing austerity policies

This chapter identifies the key lessons from organising and action against austerity policies and challenges to the neoliberal transformation of public services and welfare states. Austerity measures continue, so new lessons will continue to be learnt.

### Private sector failure – public bear the cost

The financial crisis was caused by the failure of markets and deregulation. It was a private sector failure, not a sovereign debt crisis caused by excessive government spending. Neoliberal ideology and values (such as free trade, competition, debt-driven consumerism, tax cuts for the wealthy, deregulation and privatisation) underpinned economic policies and attitudes.

National and local demonstrations and strikes were mainly targeted at governments that chose deep public spending cuts, job losses and pay cuts and other economic austerity policies. Conservative governments, business, and right wing interests blame the political party previously in power for the crisis and divert attention from financial market failure.

Austerity in the bailout countries, Spain, Greece, Portugal, Ireland and Cypress, imposed by the troika – the International Monetary Fund, the European Central Bank and the European Commission – required governments to adhere to a strict policy implementation timetable. Opposition to these policies had to confront global institutions, business interests and conservative parties, not just their respective government.

Poor, working and middle class families have borne the brunt of austerity policies in Europe and North America. The wealthy have not contributed a larger share, corporate welfare has been expanded and only Iceland jailed bankers for their role causing the financial crisis. Austerity measures include public sector wage and pension cuts and large job losses, yet public sector workers are often vilified for being 'better off' than private sector workers.

Governments in bailout countries succumbed to the interests of capital as they adhered to the terms set by the troika. The phased release of funds has been dependent on regular inspection visits by troika officials to determine progress and adherence to the bailout terms, a fundamental erosion of democratic governance.

National elections in many European countries after 2008 often resulted in conservative parties gaining power with mandates to implement austerity policies. They accelerated implementation of neoliberal policies, increased regulation of trade unions and curtailed civil liberties. In addition, extreme right wing organisations exploited the financial crisis and austerity to increased electoral support, for example, Golden Dawn in Greece.

Austerity measures make people angry but they also create fear and insecurity, which makes industrial and community action more difficult to organise. Job losses and a fear of unemployment and wage cuts, on top of high levels of credit card, mortgage and student debt, together with negative housing equity were barriers to organising. In addition, many households have sought to save to reduce debt, minimise the loss of household income and reduce expenditure. Many communities lose young, skilled people who emigrate from Ireland to Australia and North America, and from Spain and Portugal to South America and to other European countries. The need for broad alliances to oppose austerity has been hampered by claims of 'privileged' public sector workers promulgated by business, media and right-wing populism, for example in Canada, Ireland and Britain. These claims divide the better organised from the less well organised and drag public sector terms and conditions down to those in the private sector instead of lifting private to public sector standards.

## Pre-crisis flaws exposed

The financial crisis exposed flaws and fault lines that existed in each country prior to 2008. These flaws had been obscured by economic growth, enthusiasm for neoliberal economic policies, deregulation and unsustainable consumer borrowing.

Action strategies had to be drawn up under different conditions, for example, the scale of the housing and property market collapse was more severe in the US, Spain and

Ireland. The crisis exposed new vulnerabilities and imposed new demands on financially weak US cities as long-term economic and demographic change accelerated.

This period also highlighted a number of weaknesses in trade union organisation and strategies, such as the continuing loss of private sector trade union membership, the relationship with social democratic parties that embraced neoliberalism, and the failure to develop meaningful and sustainable alliances with community and civil society organisations. It meant traditional defensive strategies that focused on trying to influence public policies and/or delay/obstruct implementation had limited effect in austerity conditions.

## Cultural and political differences

Cultural as well as structural, institutional and electoral factors influence the adoption of action strategies in each country, which should be taken into account in the analysis, comparison, and transfer of national responses.

For example, despite Greece and Spain having similar background conditions and severity of austerity, there are differences in their resistance strategies. Andronikidou and Kovras (2012) identify two reasons:

> *'First, it shows how the Greek transition to democracy shaped a political 'culture of sympathy' to acts of resistance against the state. Second, it notes the mechanisms through which daily practices of resistance have become institutionalised and permeated Greek culture. It concludes that the cultivation of a political culture of sympathy has become a 'winning formula' adopted by vocal minorities who deploy unlawful protests. Equally, early socialisation into unlawful practices creates the conditions for the public to turn a blind eye to the use of violence. In Spain, by contrast, there is no such tolerance of violence.'*

## Post-austerity conditions

Austerity measures will continue for many more years. Long after countries formally exit bailout programmes, they will remain under European Central Bank supervision. Much will depend on economic performance and 'growth', levels of debt reduction, taxation policies and shifts in political control. UK Prime Minister David Cameron recently announced that the government would seek a 'leaner, more efficient state' on a permanent basis and has no intention of resuming public spending once debt levels have been reduced (The Guardian, 2013).

'Reforms' will not be reversed in economies or in the public sector. There are no plans to restore wages, pensions and public spending cuts other than proposals to restore 'growth', reduce unemployment and tackle loan sharks. Nor is there an indication that financialising, personalising, marketising and privatising public services and state assets will be reversed. In fact, these and other structural changes including radical reductions in public expenditure on services, further cuts in corporate taxation and 'reform' of labour markets are being further embedded. Private finance of services and public infrastructure is increasing as Public Private Partnership legislation and programmes are established in more countries.

***Political change*** – Labour and social democratic parties were embroiled in implementing austerity in the early stages of the crisis, for example, the UK and Spain, or in a coalition in Ireland, before conservative parties were elected.

Austerity enabled opposition parties to be highly critical of governments. It concealed the degree of political consensus between the main political parties regarding the overall management of the economy, public services and the welfare state. The 15M and Occupy movements gained traction in part because of the high level of disillusionment with traditional political parties, the lack of principles and apathy to greed and corruption.

***Power conceded*** is never handed back. Despite some successes, trade union, community and social movements could not lever sufficient power to force the state and capital to share the burden of austerity, despite widespread resistance in many countries. The combination of austerity and neoliberal policies will make it harder to organise and mobilise workers and communities. Furthermore, corporate interests will continue to try to reduce the power of trade unions and to restrict civil and community action and involvement.

***Alternative demands*** at demonstrations, marches and occupations to date included: 'keep out the troika'; 'reverse wage and pension cuts'; 'reinstate public spending cuts'; 'tax the rich, not the poor'; 'cancel the debt'; 'resignation of government'; 'progressive tax system', 'nationalise the banks'; 'stop privatisation'; and the demand for 'real democracy'.

Initial demands were mainly defensive – 'stop the cuts' – but changed from 2011 to reflect greater community and social movement involvement and the realisation that defensive demands alone were having very limited effect. The troika and government imposition of austerity measures further exposes the limitations of current forms of representation, accountability and transparency. The need to address financial reform, progressive taxation, public investment, democratic governance, transparency, the public sector and welfare state was widely recognised, yet specific demands and policies rarely got beyond broad brush statements in campaigns.

This has contributed to a limited trade union challenge to neoliberal transformation in the public sector, in particular to competition and markets. It is most evident in the UK where new pathways to privatisation have been created by financialising, personalising, marketising public services to consolidate neoliberal transformation (Whitfield, 2012a).

*'... the existence of sweeping popular movements, although it may well be a historical phenomenon, does not by itself furnish a political vision. The reason for this is that what cements a movement on the basis of individual affects is always of a negative character: the sort of thing that proceeds from abstract negations, like 'down with capitalism', or 'stop the layoffs', or 'no to austerity', or 'down with the European troika', which have strictly no other effect than provisionally soldering the movement with the negative frailty of its affects; as for more specific negations, since their target is precise and they bring together different strata of the population'* (Badiou, p. 45).

## Key responses in Europe and North America 2008-2013

The main austerity measures in the bailout conditions and austerity policies in other countries are summarised in Table 3, together with the main action strategies used to oppose those policies.

**Table 3: Main Austerity Measures and Action Strategies**

| AUSTERITY MEASURES | ACTION STRATEGIES |
|---|---|
| *Dispossession* | Strikes and industrial action |
| Public spending cuts | Demonstrations, marches and rallies |
| Outsourcing and privatisation | Occupations of public spaces |
| Pay cuts and pension changes | Sit-ins at banks and company head offices |
| Tax increases | Mass mobilisations at parliaments |
| Closure of services and facilities | Picketing and lobbying institutions and meetings |
| Increased tuition fees and charges | Eviction and road blockades |
| Mortgage foreclosures and evictions | Direct action against corporate tax avoidance |
| Welfare state benefit cuts | Public rallies, meetings and assemblies |
| Bankruptcy of cities with cuts to services, jobs and pensions | Exposing impact of outsourcing and privatisation. |
| *Neoliberal policies and corporate welfare* | Living wage campaigns targeting specific employers |
| Private finance Public Private Partnerships | |
| Marketisation of public services | |
| Bank and corporate bailouts | |
| More stringent regulation of trade unions | |
| Corporate welfare and tax reductions | |

The key responses to austerity in Europe and North America during the period 2008-2013 are summarised in Table 4, sourced from international and national organisations, press releases, journal articles, web sites and media.

## Table 4: Key responses in Europe and North America 2008-2013

| DATE | SUMMARY OF KEY EVENTS |
|---|---|
| 2008 | |
| October 22 | 15,000 pensioners & 10,000 students protest in Dublin against withdrawal of medical cards and increased student fees. |
| 2009 | |
| January 3-26 | Demonstrations at Iceland's parliament in Reykjavik to protest at bank bailout terms. |
| February 21 | Irish Congress of Trade Unions 100,000 march in Dublin against pensions levy and cuts. |
| November 24 | 250,000 public sector workers national strike in Ireland against pay cuts. |
| 2010 | |
| March 6 | First Icelandic referendum on repayment of bank debts defeated 93% voting against. |
| May 5 | National strike and large demonstrations in Athens and Thessaloniki against bailout terms, spending cuts and tax increases. |
| October 26 | UK Uncut direct action launched in London and spread to other cities. |
| November 3 | 40,000 students march in Dublin against increased tuition fees, cuts and emigration |
| 2011 | |
| February 14 - June 16 | Series of strikes and mass opposition to State of Wisconsin anti-union legislation, big increases in public sector healthcare and pension contributions and budget cuts. |
| February 23 | 100,000 Athens demonstration after Greek government told to accelerate austerity |
| March 26 | 250,000 march in London against austerity policies organised by Trade Union Congress. |
| April 9 | Second Icelandic referendum on repayment of bank debt defeated 60% voted against. |
| May 15 | Large demonstrations in Madrid and other Spanish cities and emergence of 15M community organizing movement. Occupation of Puerta del Sol spreads to other cities. |
| May 25 to August 7 | Anti-austerity protests and sit-ins in several cities in Greece organized by Indignant Citizens Movement. |
| June 28-29 | General strike in Greece against austerity |
| June 30 | UK civil servants, teachers & municipal workers one-day strike against pension changes. |
| October 13-15 | 100,000 surrounded parliament in Lisbon against Portugal's 2012 budget and wage cuts |
| October 15 | Global day of action in 900 cities in support of Occupy movement, 200,000 in Rome. |
| November 16 | 20,000 students march in Dublin to oppose reintroduction of student fees. |
| November 12 | National demonstration with 180,000 in Lisbon opposing Portugal's austerity measures. |
| November 27 | 100,000 march in Dublin against austerity measures. |
| November 30 | 2m public sector workers one-day UK strike over pension changes. Anti-austerity demonstrations in 25 countries called by European Federation of Public Service Unions. |
| 2012 | |
| February 10 | Over 100,000 at Lisbon rally against IMF and austerity policies. |
| February 12 | Greek parliament approves further cuts as 500,000 surround parliament |
| February 13 | Quebec student strike against tuition fee increases commences, 300,000 on strike (75% of students) by March 22 when over 200,000 marched in Montreal. Increases abandoned in May and Parti Liberal du Quebec lost election. |

| | |
|---|---|
| May 19 | Blockupy Frankfurt 4-day action against European Central Bank ends with 25,000 march. |
| May 22 | 400,000 march in Montreal in support of student strike and against austerity. |
| September 15 | Large 'Screw the Troika' demonstrations across Portugal. |
| October 18 | General strike in Greece with rallies in many cities against draft budget |
| November 7 | 80,000 demonstration & 48 hour general strike in Greece against €13.5bn (£11.1bn) austerity cuts. |
| November 14 | European Trade Union Confederation day of union struggle in 23 countries; general strikes in Spain and Portugal, strikes in Italy, France, Belgium and Greece; large marches – 150,000 in Rome and London, 100,000 in Dublin and in 130 cities in France. |
| 2013 | |
| March 2 | 1.5m participate in 'Screw the Troika' protest, Portugal, 200,000 at Finance Ministry, Lisbon. |
| March 14 | Europe-wide rallies organized by European Federation of Public Service Unions. |
| May 31 & June 1 | 'People Against the Troika' day of action called by coalitions in Spain and Portugal with demonstrations in 99 cities in 12 countries. The previous day 3,000 Blockupy activists close the European Central Bank in Frankfurt. |
| June 11 | Public TV/radio network, ERT, closed by government then occupied for 5 months. |
| June 15 | 8,000 doctors and medical staff march in Paris against budget cuts in health services. |
| June 22 | 4,000 attend Peoples Assembly in London. |
| June 27 | General strike in Portugal against austerity policies. |
| September 29 | 50,000 at Save the National Health Service march in Manchester. |
| October 19 | Large marches in Lisbon, Porto and other cities opposed to 2014 budget cuts. |
| October 23 | High response to national public education strike in Spain called by students, parents and unions against budget cuts, larger classes, and tuition fee increases. |
| November 6 | General strike in Greece against visit of troika. |

Note: The summary excludes demonstrations at G8, G20 and IMF/World Bank meetings and May Day marches in 2008-2013. They focused on a broader agenda and not solely in opposition to austerity policies.

# Significant struggles against Austerity

This section examines several important struggles against austerity in Europe and North America between 2008 and 2013. They are by necessity selective, but cover a range of action strategies to confront public spending cuts, pay and collective bargaining, foreclosures and evictions, hospital closures, tuition fee increases, privatisation and new organising strategies.

## Action against public spending cuts and privatisation

### Wisconsin uprising

In February 2011 the Republican Governor of Wisconsin introduced a Combined Budget Repair Bill to rescind public sector collective bargaining rights (excluding police and fire-fighters) together with annual union re-certification. The Bill planned to increase public sector workers health and pension costs by up to 13% and cut US$1.25bn (£753m) from public education, health and a raft of social programmes for poor families and expand private charter schools.

Between 15 February and 12 March 2011 a series of demonstrations, strikes and occupations in Madison, the state capital, each involved between 10,000 – 100,000 public and private sector trade unionists, students and supporters (Morris, 2012, Collins, 2012 and Borsos, 2012). The Capitol building was occupied for many days. The Governor was soon forced to separate the bill proposals – the State Assembly approved the budget on 25 February and the collective bargaining legislation on 10 March, despite the absence of 14 Democratic senators who had left the state to try to prevent the vote. Two days later they returned to Madison to a large rally.

The emphasis shifted to petition for recall elections. The April election to choose a State Supreme Court justice led to the former Republican leader in the state legislature winning the election after 14,000 votes were 'found'. A 5-week recount could not prove they were fraudulent, so the court retained a conservative majority.

Six Republican and three Democratic senators faced recall elections in August 2011 and although two Republicans lost their seats, the party retained controlled of the Senate. The following year over a million signatures were collected to force a recall election of Governor Walker. He won a 53.1% majority in June 2012 over the Democrat Mayor of Milwaukee. Walker's campaign outspent the Democrats by 7:1 mainly due to out-of-state conservative supporters such as the Koch brothers (New York Times, 2012, Nichols, 2012a and Dinovella, 2012). Exit polls revealed 36% of union households voted for Walker! (Nichols, 2012b).

Many important lessons were learnt from the creative, militant and well-organised action. It drew support from across North America and overseas, but also exposed strategic failures:

- Some trade union leaders concentrated their demands on public sector collective bargaining rights and did not address the budget proposals and wider community interests – 'it's not about the money' (Henwood, 2012a and Rothschild, 2012).

- Large numbers of teachers were involved – 24 schools districts were closed in the first week of action and whilst there was support for a general strike, one was never called and would have been illegal under labour laws.

- No attempts were made for any meaningful, even symbolic, democratic decision-making during the demonstrations and occupations (Rothschild, 2012).

- The large 12 March rally launched the recall strategy and marked the end of demonstrations which '... *diffused the protests geographically and emotionally ... destroyed the lesson that you can exercise power outside of the electoral arena ... fed the assumption that the Democratic Party was the be all and end all ... it took mass power off the streets when it was needed'* (Rothschild, 2012) such as the Supreme Court decision and the June 2011 budget process.

- The recall campaign had limited effect. Democratic candidates made no mention of collective bargaining in their election addresses and they failed to gain control of the Senate (Cole and Gasper, 2012 and Morris, 2012). The Democratic candidate, the Mayor of Milwaukee, had lost to Walker in the 2010 Governorship election. *'Democrats struggled with the message, trying to transition the radicalism of the Capitol protest of 2011 ... months of soft messaging about important issues – from education to voting rights – took some edge off the movement messaging that had defined protests and petitioning for the recall'* (Nichols, 2012c). The secretary-treasurer of the National Union of Healthcare Workers concluded:

  *'Nichols's analysis begs the question: will the institutional labor movement ever depart from the formulaic, stale, poll and focus-group tested, watered-down messaging regarding "middle-class values" and actually defend in a clear and concise way "working class" interests? Wisconsin workers in February and March 2011 spoke the language of class. Will their so-called leaders ever have the courage to do the same?'* (Borsis, 2012).

- The 2010 US Supreme Court 'Citizens United' decision barred the federal government from restricting political expenditure by corporations, trade unions and political action committees (Center for Public Integrity, 2012). This has enabled corporate interests to target opposition to free market policies. The Republican strategy was to blame trade unions for low quality services being delivered in the poorest neighbourhoods and claimed public sector salary and benefits were 'too generous'. This requires the labour movement to organise and agitate on behalf of entire communities (Henwood, 2012b; Rothschild, 2012; Borsos, 2012; Morris, 2012).

- The elimination of automatic payroll deduction of membership dues and annual votes requiring majority membership vote, to recertify a union, had an immediate impact. Some unions decided not to seek certification, made alternative arrangements to collect dues and have reduced union staffing levels as union membership declined. Public sector unions lost 50,000 members with the Wisconsin state workers union density declining from 50% to 37% and the state's overall union density from 15.2% to 11.2% by the end of 2012 (McCartin, 2013).

**Quebec student strike succeeds**

A student strike began on 13 February 2012 and by mid-March 300,000 of the 400,000 student body were on strike against a 75% increase in tuition fees by 2017. The government claimed the increase was necessary because of budget shortfall, but was part of a policy to increase existing fees for public services and introduce new ones. On 22 March 2012 over 200,000 students, trade unionists and people from a wide range of community organisations marched in Montréal, the largest in Quebec's history.

The strike and demonstrations continued and student organisations re-opened negotiations with the government, which made some concessions. However, students at every post-secondary institution rejected the agreement. Two weeks later the Minister of Education resigned. The government passed emergency Law 78 on 18 May, which suspended the current academic year, enabled the police to ban assemblies at universities and limited university worker's right to strike. Four days later 400,000 people marched through Montréal, after which the government withdrew from negotiations. Students voted to defy the law and the march was a public challenge to the draconian measures. Police made 3,387 arrests between February and September 2012 (Solty, 2012). The ruling Parti Liberal du Quebec was defeated in an early election in September that year. The new government froze tuition fees and rescinded the emergency legislation.

The student strike became Canada's 'maple spring' and provided some crucial lessons for resistance to austerity:

- The key student body, the Coalition large de l'Association pour une solidarite syndicale etudiante (CLASSE) rejected lobbying and organised through local plenary assemblies and a national delegate assembly. It was committed to grassroots mobilisation (Solty, 2012), grounded in democracy, militancy and audacity (Lafrance and Sears, 2013). CLASSE is one of four Quebec student associations with 65 local associations and 100,000 members (Camfield, 2012).

- Students *'... formed strike committees, held general assemblies, organised alternative education events and built alliances with organisations and social movements outside of post-secondary institutions'* (Solty, 2012). It also raised questions about forms of democratic governance and the form of post-secondary education (Lafrance and Sears, 2013).

- *'... students took their struggle off campus and carried out blockades of government offices, courthouses, bank buildings, bridges and other targets. Students also marched in support of locked-out Rio Tinto aluminum smelter workers in the town of Alma, joined with other groups protesting austerity measures and protested the government's plan to "develop" Northern Quebec, which is opposed by indigenous people and environmentalists'* (Camfield, 2012).

- The 'Red-Hand Coalition' of 125 organisations ranging from education and healthcare trade unions, poverty initiatives, environmental and community organisations had a vital role in coordinating support for the student strike. This large coalition had formed three years earlier to oppose Quebec's budget cuts and austerity measures.

- *'... the Quebec student strike would not have proceeded so successfully without the Red-Hand-Coalition's networking of social struggles ... a spontaneous protest only becomes fully effective if a strong organization and a broad alliance of social forces have prepared the ground for its emergence'* (Solty, 2012).

- Students succeeded by ensuring tuition fees were not just a 'student issue' or an isolated austerity measure, but a wider struggle against imposing austerity measures on working people. The strike was widely supported by teachers and support staff (Democracy Now, 2012).

- CLASSE organised to win a strike mandate in the preceding two years through assemblies, days of action, demonstrations, petitions and leaflets. It planned for the strike and drew on lessons from previous student action against tuition increases.

**Other action against austerity in education**

In other countries students and teachers have taken action against tuition fee increases, job losses and cuts to campus services as state and local government imposed austerity measures.

The university of California imposed a 32% tuition fee increase in 2009, which led to a series of occupations, sit-ins, rallies and demonstrations. Disciplinary action against students led to fewer and smaller protests in 2010. But by April 2011 there were ten simultaneous occupations and days of action at 23 state universities and 112 community colleges (Levenson, 2011).

A nine-day strike in 2012 by Chicago public schools teachers resulted in the mayor signing an agreement that avoided the closure of 120 schools. The first teacher strike for 25 years in the city was widely supported by parents, students and community organisations. The mayor has since proposed closing fifty schools in inner neighbourhoods and continues to cut school budgets in a drive to increase non-union, privately run charter schools. The Chicago teachers union has organised mass protests and some schools have been saved from closure (Yates, 2013).

The shift from public schools to US charter schools, UK academies and free schools in Sweden and the UK and the privatisation of universities and colleges is increasingly the focus of protest by student organisations, education sector trade unions and social movements.

**Spain's Movement of Mortgage Victims**

Anti-foreclosure and eviction campaigns in Spain, the Plataforma de Afectados por la

Hipoteca (PAH) have organised local resistance to evictions with national action calling for a change in government and bank policies. PAH began organising in Barcelona in 2009 and then grew rapidly as part of the 15M movement in May 2011, as banks have enforced 420,000 foreclosures and 220,000 evictions in the last six years. It had 160 local organisations by 2013 (Lamarca, 2013a and 2013b). Twenty per cent or 5.6 million homes are unoccupied in Spain.

PAH has organised blockades to stop evictions and has organised the occupation of empty homes and buildings by families evicted due to foreclosure. It also occupied banks to demand debt forgiveness. Firemen and locksmiths in a Coruna, Catalonia and Madrid have refused to assist in evictions. Foreclosures and evictions not only increase homelessness and impose personal financial losses, but unoccupied housing results in a spiral of neighbourhood degeneration, job losses and falling house prices.

PAH campaigned for legislative change to enable people to surrender key and occupation to banks and be released from continuing financial liability. It prepared draft new laws and collected 1.4m signatures in support. Spain's draconian mortgage laws allow banks to claim full repayment of debt, including any difference in value and legal costs, even after evicting residents (Sutherland, 2013).

The government ignored the PAH proposals and introduced its own very limited measures in April 2013. Only households in extreme hardship that met strict conditions would have their eviction orders frozen for two years. The European Court of Justice had earlier ruled that previous procedures violated EU consumer regulations (Buck, 2013).

PAH organised demonstrations in Spanish towns and cities in February 2013. It intensified the campaign with *escrache* or unmasking demonstrations at Popular Party politician's homes to try to persuade them to support the legislation. The government has made arrests and threatened large fines in attempts to discredit the PAH. But the grassroots organisation has wide support – a poll found 78% of Spaniards supported the escrache action (Alvarez et al, 2013).

**Organising against US foreclosures and evictions**

Although us foreclosures and evictions declined from the 2009 peak (see Chapter 1), they are concentrated in particular neighbourhoods and have led to community resistance. Standing Against Foreclosure and Eviction (Seattle), Occupy Homes Minneapolis, Anti-Eviction Campaign (Chicago) and Detroit Eviction Defense, are examples of community resistance to foreclosures and evictions. Action has included rapid response teams and community pickets to stop evictions; eviction free zones; re-occupying homes; opposing auctions; sit ins and demonstrations at banks, mortgage companies and public agencies to prevent foreclosures; exposing the scale and consequences of foreclosures; launching legal action against banks and community support in legal cases; building community alliances and links with campaigns in other cities. Buffalo City Council withdrew US$45m (£27.1m) from JP Morgan Chase bank in response to its foreclosure policies and several smaller towns have withdrawn accounts from Chase and Wells Fargo banks in response to demands from anti-foreclosure and eviction campaigns (The Huffington Post, 2012).

**Madrid hospitals anti-privatisation campaign and legal action**
Fifty thousand people took part in the eleventh 'white tide' march of healthcare workers and community and trade union supporters in Madrid to celebrate the Madrid Supreme Court decision to suspend the privatisation of six hospitals, four specialist centres and 27 community health centres in September 2013. One of the campaign organisers, the Association of Medical Specialists, had taken legal action to suspend the public tender issued earlier in May. The Madrid government had selected three private health management companies to operate the hospitals, but finally abandoned the plan in February 2014. The regional health commissioner resigned (Marcos, 2014).

The Associacion Para la Defensa de la Sanidad Publica de Madrid (Association for the Defence of Public Healthcare), and other groups, organised demonstrations on the third Sunday every month after the regional government agreed the 10-year outsourcing plan in December 2012. An initial strike of doctors and nurses in late 2012 failed to stop the proposal and was followed by five one-day strikes in May and June 2013 (non-urgent care) in the city's 34 hospitals and many health centres. The demonstrations and strikes have been widely supported – opinion polls show 70% of people oppose healthcare privatisation (Reuters, 2013a). The campaign also organised rallies and lobbied the Madrid Regional Assembly, mass meetings, sit-ins, petitions and 14km marches from the Hospital del Henares, Coslada to Madrid (Equal Times, 2013).

Building wide community support under the 'public health: don't sell, defend it' banner, the organising of health workers in a range of action strategies, critical analysis of the government's proposals and legal action were critical factors in the success of the campaign.

**London's Lewisham Hospital campaign**
The UK government appointed a 'special administrator' to take over the South London Healthcare Trust in July 2012. He proposed closing accident and emergency, children's wards, critical care, emergency, complex surgery units and maternity services at Lewisham hospital. The empty buildings would be sold for £17m. The plan was to channel patients to the Queen Elizabeth Hospital, burdened with high Private Finance Initiative (PFI) debt. *'It is the PFI that is being bailed out, not the clinical services which people in south-east London depend on. This prioritising of debt repayment over service provision is, in our view, the principal reason that Lewisham hospital, without a significant PFI, was chosen to take the brunt of the cuts'* (Save Lewisham Campaign, 2013).

The Save Lewisham Campaign of patients, doctors, nurses, other healthcare workers, trade unions, political and community organisations built strong support locally and across London. 15,000 marched in November 2012 followed by a march of 25,000 in January 2013. Rallies, mass meetings, workplace protests and public meetings were followed by High Court action in July 2013, which ruled that the Secretary of State had acted unlawfully in announcing closure of A&E and maternity units. The campaign group 38 Degrees raised donations from its national membership, plus local financial support from Millwall Football Club and many others to finance the judicial review.

The Secretary of State for Health appealed, but this was rejected the following October. The government had earlier added a last minute amendment to the Care Bill, which if passed would *'... legalise much more widespread use of fast-track hospital closures'* (Molloy, 2013).

Both the Madrid and Lewisham, London Campaigns won important victories and intend to continue organising and taking action to address wider issues and the threat that legal success may be reversed by respective governments.

**Privatisation defeated by Stroud Against the Cuts**

A concerted campaign by Stroud Against the Cuts successfully stopped NHS Gloucestershire from outsourcing eight community hospitals and health services when the Gloucestershire Primary Care Trust was abolished in 2013. The eighteen-month campaign included a high court challenge against Gloucestershire Primary Care Trust's failure to fully examine options for the services. A February 2012 court order halted the planned outsourcing and in May, health ministers and the Trust conceded that creating an NHS Trust was an option and there was no legal requirement for putting the services out to tender.

The court order also required NHS Gloucestershire to consult with staff and the public, which resulted in 91% of staff and 96% of the public voting for services to be run by an NHS Trust (Stroud Against the Cuts, 2012). Gloucestershire Care Services NHS Trust was formed in April 2013 and employs 2,800 skilled staff and manages a further 800 adult social care staff on behalf of Gloucestershire County Council.

In addition to legal action, the campaign held marches, organised petitions, held public meetings, lobbied NHS meetings and was widely supported by NHS staff and unions and the national campaign Keep Our NHS Public.

**Greece – militant action against austerity**

A series of general strikes and large demonstrations were held at each round of austerity measures in early 2010, followed by similar action at each parliamentary debate on budget cuts, bail-out terms and visits by the troika after the two bailouts. The economic crisis worsened as austerity policies imposed a downward spiral of cuts, job losses, hardship and political turmoil. Syriza, a left coalition, won 71 seats and 27% share of the votes in the June 2012 national election and is the formal opposition.

Strikes and demonstrations were organised by particular sectors. For example, teachers unions reported a 90% turnout for a strike on 16 September 2013 that began a week-long series of strikes by public sector workers. A two-month strike of university administrative workers at the University of Athens and National Technical University in 2013 stopped classes, exams and enrolment. University budgets had been cut by 40% and 60% respectively and the government planned a big reduction in support staff. Two-day strikes at Thessaloniki universities and colleges followed in September 2013.

Thessaloniki's White Tower and Heraklion's Eleftherias squares were occupied for several weeks in 2011. Several protests in Athens' Syntagma Square that summer were ended by riot police, resulting in hundreds of protestors being injured.
2,300 journalists, technicians, news editors and support staff of ERT, the public broadcasting TV and radio network, were laid off by the Greek government in June 2013. They began a five-month occupation of the ERT centre and provided a 24-hour service until an early morning raid by riot police in November.

The harsh social and economic consequences led to the provision of mutual support and solidarity services. They include food kitchens, farmers markets, free markets to exchange clothing and other essentials, solidarity clinics for medical treatment, free lessons by high school teachers and legal support to help people avoid losing their homes, electricity and water (Simpson, 2013). These initiatives have become an important activity in parallel with industrial and political action. Greece solidarity campaigns have been established in many countries.

There is a danger that austerity conditions lead to the emergence of opportunistic right wing organisations. The fascist Golden Dawn party received 13% of the vote in the June 2012 election and has 18 members of parliament. An anti-fascist hip-hop artist was murdered by a Golden Dawn supporter in September 2013, and numerous attacks have been made on immigrants and asylum seekers (Syllas, 2013).

**Iceland stops repayment of bank debt**

Shortly after the collapse of three Icelandic banks in 2008 and deteriorating economic conditions a series of noisy demonstrations of between 2,000 – 7,000 people were regularly held at the Parliament in Reykjavik between October 2008 and January 2009. They surrounded the building with the intention of preventing or disrupting parliamentary meetings. There were many clashes with riot police and arrests. The right-wing Independence Party government resigned in late January 2009. The Social Democratic Alliance and Left-Green Movement formed an interim government and won a majority of seats in the April election.

The first Icesave Referendum was held in early 2010 after Britain and the Netherlands demanded repayment of depositor's losses in the foreign subsidiary of the collapsed Landsbanki Bank. The President of Iceland invoked the 1944 constitution to hold a referendum in which 98% voted that taxpayers should not bail out the banks. Another referendum was held in 2011 after the Icelandic Parliament agreed to a repayment plan, but this was again voted down at another referendum with a smaller, but clear, majority. The UK and Netherlands governments paid €6.7bn (£5.5bn) compensation to 425,000 Icesave savers and took legal action against Iceland for failing to meet its compensation obligations, but a European Free Trade Area court dismissed this case in January 2012.

Four Icelandic bankers were jailed for up to 5.5 years in December 2013 for fraud and market manipulation in the collapsed Kaupthing Bank. A year earlier two bankers in the failed Glitnir Bank were jailed for nine months for fraud (Financial Times, 2012a).

**Portland, USA, action against cuts**

Over four hundred trade union and community representatives challenged the need for US$25m (£15.1m) savings in an April 2013 budget hearing in the preparation of the Portland, Oregon, 2013-2014 budget. They gave evidence opposing the cuts and protested the Council's refusal to discuss alternatives to austerity. At a subsequent hearing it emerged that US$3.5m (£2.1m) was 'found' and the loss of 142 full-time equivalent jobs reduced to 25 people through a voluntary retirement incentive programme. An alternative plan for a progressive county income tax, a progressive business tax in place of the current flat rate scheme and restructure of the Portland Development Commission by two academic economists was rejected.

> *'The grassroots struggle over the city budget in 2013 helped to spread the popularity of such an approach and established a network of union and community members who are willing to unite around it. By focusing on building unity around concrete revenue-raising proposals, by exposing how budget priorities are set and how they hurt our communities, and by organizing to expand our movement, we will be better able to face the challenges coming our way in 2014'* (Solidarity Against Austerity, 2013).

## Opposition to privatisation

This section refers to action taken specifically against the privatisation of state owned corporations as distinct from it being an integral part of campaigns against austerity. It also only deals with austerity related privatisation since 2008 (see Whitfield, 2010 and 2012a for analysis of privatisation).

US and UK governments re-privatised some bank and other financial institution assets nationalised after 2008. The UK sold a 6% stake in Lloyds bank in September 2013 but still retains a 39% stake and 81% stake in Royal Bank of Scotland. Germany is selling DEPFRA Bank Plc (Dublin based) a European Commission requirement following the German government bailout of €10bn (£8.2bn) capital and €124bn (£101.6bn) liquidity guarantees during the period 2008-2010 (Moody's, 2013). There has been some criticism, but little resistance to these sales.

All five bailout countries are being forced to privatise a range of public assets. However, there have been relatively few assets privatised to date, such as lotteries (Ireland) and land and buildings. Greece has privatised a controlling stake in the gaming company OPAP and sold land and buildings in several areas and overseas. The OPAP sale to Emma Delta Consortium of Czech, Russian, Slovak and Greek investors is currently being investigated by the Athens prosecutor (Financial Times, 2014). More contentious assets sales are in progress or are part of longer-term programmes that will extend beyond bailout programmes. The sale of Thessaloniki Water in Greece and Ireland's Bord Gais Energy are underway with increasing opposition. Privatisation has continued in other European countries such as UK's sale of a majority stake in Royal Mail in 2013. But some assets have been re-nationalised and re-municipalised, for example in France, Germany and the UK since 2008. Public ownership of the economic and social infrastructure is vitally important. Returning the management and control of schools, hospitals, council housing, public transport, roads, water and energy to the public sector is vitally important. Water in Paris and Berlin has returned to public provision, London transport PPPs collapsed and some local services have returned to in-house provision. But these important developments do not represent a 'wave' of re-nationalisation when compared with the increasing rate of outsourcing and privatisation.

At the local level two UK campaigns to prevent large-scale outsourcing had very different outcomes. Edinburgh City Council terminated the procurement of three strategic partnerships for corporate and transactional services, integrated facilities management and environmental services between November 2011 and January 2012. Trade unions had campaigned for two years for in-house improvement plans and against privatisation. High levels of trade union membership and Edinburgh's political control were significant factors. The City Council had been a Liberal Democrat/Scottish National Party coalition since 2007 with four parties, including Labour and Conservative, having between 16-11 seats and the Greens three seats.

In contrast, the London Borough of Barnet embarked on a mass outsourcing of services in 2008. Trade unions, in particular UNISON, challenged and criticised each stage with support from the European Services Strategy Unit. However, their proposals and comments were largely ignored, despite detailed critical analysis and making the case for an alternative service improvement strategy. Staff took industrial action at a key stage of the procurement process. The Conservatives with a 15-seat majority proceeded to outsource planning, regulatory and corporate services in two contracts worth £475m with nearly 800 staff. The council also outsourced parking and transferred adult learning and physical disability services with 172 staff to a local authority trading company.

A vibrant Barnet Public Service Alliance community campaign began in autumn 2010. With few divisions in Conservative ranks and/or managers willing to break from neoliberal management practice, it was increasingly evident that this was not a 'local' problem, nor could it be 'resolved' locally. Sixty-five PPP strategic partnership services contracts have been signed in the UK in the last decade with a contract value of £14.4bn and 28,600 jobs, plus fifty highway services and waste management contracts (Whitfield, 2014).

**Germany: blockade of the European Central Bank**

The European Central Bank headquarters in Frankfurt was blockaded and closed on 31 May 2013 by 3,000 Blockupy activists, including many from other European countries. A similar action a year earlier was thwarted by a citywide ban on protests and police roadblocks. This time Blockupy marched to the bank at 5am. After the ECB closed the bank, they marched to the city centre and blocked the main shopping street to highlight low wages and temporary work. The following day, 15,000 marched to the ECB headquarters, but were stopped by police demanding identification checks. Many were injured and arrested after the police used tear gas.

Both demonstrations were preceded by four days of meetings and debates on pan-European issues and tactics. Die Linke, Germany's largest left-wing party, supported the protests, but '*... most trade unions were completely absent as well as other large organisations of the reformist left'* (Principe and Thun, 2013).

**Ireland limited by social partnership**

A social partnership between unions, employers and the state led to a muted response and lack of leadership in challenging draconian austerity policies. Social partnerships commenced in 1987 with three-year national agreements covering pay restraint, public sector staffing and procedures and included trade unions support for PPPS. The employers withdrew in 2009, but the following year the Irish Congress of Trade Unions (ICTU) and the government signed a Public Service Agreement that included large pay and pension cuts, job losses and increased efficiency measures.

Social partnership is deeply embedded and has led to reduced member involvement in unions and accelerated the trend towards 'business unionism' (Allen, 2013 and Erne, 2013). The ICTU organised marches as part of European Trade Union Confederation days of action, but little more. The prime response to austerity was to replace one partnership with another.

However, there have been several local hospital campaigns against closures that attracted large support, such as 15,000 people in Waterford (10 February, 2012), 7,000 in Navan (30 October 2010) and 8,000 in Roscommon on 14 august, 2010).

**Other EU countries**

Demonstrations were not confined to the bailout countries and other E15 countries. In Bulgaria, demonstrations in early 2013 were sparked by high energy prices, which led to a general election. Within months further street protests demanded an end to political corruption (Stankova, 2013). Privatisation of emergency services in a new health bill triggered protests in 60 towns and cities in Romania in 2012, leading to the resignation of the government in February 2012 (Volintiru, 2012).

**Action in cities facing financial crisis**

Local trade unions and community organisations held marches, lobbies and pickets of council meetings and the US District Court in Detroit during the bankruptcy proceedings. More than 1,000 surrounded the bankruptcy court in October 2013 and earlier demonstrations had demanded 'no deals with banks', 'bailout cities – not banks', resignation of the emergency manager and the protection of health and pension benefits.

Meanwhile, the Chicago Teachers Union (CTU) demanded the Chicago City Council reallocate surpluses in 151 Tax Increment Financing zones and re-negotiate Bank of America toxic swap deals with the city. The CTU demonstrated at the bank's State Street branch in June 2013 – schools were paying a fixed interest rate of 5% compared to the bank's 0.42%, resulting in a loss of US$35m (£21.1m) to Chicago schools (Chicago Teachers Union, 2013 and McCartin, 2013). The CTU and Service Employees International Union and the UNITE union are part of the Grassroots Collaborative that includes low-wage service employees, the homeless, senior citizens, immigrants, peace activists, faith leaders, and residents of poor and working class neighbourhoods (http://www.thegrassrootscollaborative.org).

UK Regional Development Agencies were abolished in 2012 and 'replaced' with powerful business–led Local Enterprise Partnerships (alongside City Deals and a Single Local Growth Fund) with strategic long-term plans for economic development; transport, infrastructure and housing investment; and EU Structural and Investment Funds in England. The government also deregulated city planning and adopted Tax Increment Financing (funding building projects by borrowing against future property tax increases). There has been a muted response from trade unions and community organisations to these drastic changes.

**Free trade agreements extend austerity**

Several free trade agreements are currently being negotiated that will extend the austerity agenda through further deregulation, procurement, privatisation together with new corporate powers.

The Transatlantic Trade and Investment Partnership (TTIP), also known as the Transatlantic Free Trade Agreement (TAFTA), could roll-back financial reforms, buy-local rules, tax breaks for alternative fuels, food and product safety standards, data privacy protections and limit negotiations to reduce healthcare costs. It could massively increase corporate power through extra-judicial tribunals to protect investor rights (Corporate Europe Observatory, 2013 and Public Citizen, 2013a).

The draft Trans Pacific Partnership (TPP) includes the US and eleven Pacific Rim countries, such as Australia, Canada and Japan, and has a docking system to allow other countries to join later. The TPP extends well beyond state-owned corporations, local government purchasing, patent and other regulations. The TPP is primarily a US *'... geo-political exercise with a dual purpose: to construct a trade and investment bloc which reflects U.S. commercial interests and regulatory norms, and to counter the growing dominance of china in the Asia-Pacific region ... ultimately, the goal is to convince china to join the TPP on terms that compel Chinese reform in areas such as state-owned enterprises and currency manipulation'* (Sinclair, 2013).

The TTIP has a similar *'... investor-state enforcement system, which elevates individual corporations to equal status with sovereign nations in order to enforce privately a public treaty by demanding compensation from governments before panels of private-sector attorneys for government actions that undermine expected future profits'* (Public Citizen, 2013b). For example, the pharmaceutical firm Eli Lilly is demanding C$500m (£270m) from Canada, where courts invalidated patents on medicines that did not perform as promised. Canada is also engaged in the Canada-European Union Comprehensive Economic and Trade Agreement (CETA) negotiations to liberalise trade and procurement.

The US-Colombia Free Trade Agreement came into force in May 2012. This was after the US produced a sham 'Labor Action Plan' to appease Congressional five-year opposition given Colombia's violent treatment of trade unionists. A farmer's strike demanding suspension of the FTA in August 2013 mushroomed into a seven-week national strike of miners, teachers, truckers and students as shortages increased and prices soared. Over 200,000 people blockaded highways on the sixth day of the strike. Later twelve people were killed and over 500 injured following a violent crackdown. The government made some concessions and negotiations continue (Mather, 2013).

## New organising strategies

### Spain's 15M Movement

The Real Democracy Now Platform (Platforma Democracia Real Ya!), a grassroots organisation formed earlier in 2011 with a manifesto demanding an ethical revolution, participative democracy, the right to housing, employment, culture and health and an end to the lust for power and accumulation for the few (http://www.democraciarealya.es/manifiesto-comun/manifesto-english/).

On May 15 it organised a Madrid protest that 50,000 mainly young people participated in. A small occupation of the Puerta del Sol that evening led to heavy-handed police intervention and arrests. Thousands of people returned to the square in protest and occupations of main squares spread to other cities. A month later over one million people took part in 15M demonstrations across Spain, with 200,000 in Barcelona.

The 15M movement was deeply involved in the Movement of Mortgage Victims (see above) and redirected its activities from October 2011 to focus on activism in neighbourhoods through assemblies, coalitions and direct action. It was a bottom-up, networked approach, in direct contrast to the vertical power structures of the main parties (Elola, 2012). 15M returned to national protests on 15 May 2012, although fewer participated.

The movement grew beyond and because of delusion with the main political parties and trade unions, which represent about 17% of the workforce. However, there was an escalation in labour disputes in 2012 with two general strikes, both supported by key 15M collectives. They also supported demonstrations organised by smaller unions and inspired the 'tide' movements consisting of '*... collectives of both state employees and users in defense of public services threatened by government cuts, using a different color for each one (white for the health system, green for education, yellow for public libraries and so on ... Or the "iaioflautas"1, a collective of elderly people who are leading many actions with high media impact, mainly occupations of bank offices and public administrations'* (Cerrillo Vidal, 2013).

> *'Both the content (the call for an improvement in democratic processes) and the format of the event (with the rank-and-file overtaking the leadership in numbers and militancy) suggest that the union movement has been strongly impregnated by the agendas and demands of the 15M movement, even if this convergence has not yet been translated into the formation of a renewed, more diverse leadership or a more profound sharing of networks' (Marti, 2012).*

The 15M movement made the case for 'inclusive strikes' that engage the unemployed, students, precarious workers and all citizens, and would require new and innovative forms of social and labour protest.

**UK Uncut**

The UK Uncut movement began with demonstrations against tax dodging stores and banks such as Vodafone, HSBC, Barclays, Topshop and others in autumn 2010. It began with the closure of Vodafone's flagship store in London's Oxford Street and quickly spread to other cities using occupations and close-downs to highlight the scale of tax avoidance by individual firms and the national scale of the problem. Later Amazon, Google and Starbucks were also targeted. It was highly successful in pushing tax avoidance up the political agenda.

The strategy of linking direct action against tax avoidance with specific public spending cuts continued with a series of campaigns that included:

- Action against the big six energy companies over price increases.
- Road block protests against cuts and 'reform' of legal aid.
- A joint occupation of the headquarters of the Department for Work and Pensions

and at Atos, the outsourcing company with a contract to the company to assess whether claimants for incapacity benefits are 'fit for work', against welfare cuts.

- Occupation of high street banks to set up 'operating theatres' to highlight alternatives to cuts in the National Health Service.

- UK Uncut organises and operates through its website and social media with extensive use of video of actions to encourage similar demonstrations in other cities.

**Occupy Wall Street**

The Arab Spring, particularly in the occupation of Tahrir Square in Cairo, Egypt, inspired the occupy movement in Europe and North America. The Occupy Wall Street (OWS) occupation of Zuccotti Park began on 17 September 2011 and ended with a violent police eviction on November 15. It generated occupations not only in other cities across North America and Europe, but in small towns too. Nearly thirty per cent of California's incorporated 482 towns and cities were occupying spaces and organising events in December 2011 (University of California, Riverside, 2011).

Trade union support for the occupation was initially tentative, but delegations began arriving and offers of support and supplies increased:

> *'Union members arrived in force to support the eviction defense on October 14. Later in the day, members of OWS joined the picket line in front of Verizon [telecommunications company] headquarters. They carried signs declaring 'We are the 99%' linking worker struggles with a movement against corporate greed. Throughout the following weeks, OWS members spoke out in support movements for health care, higher education, and efforts to oppose hydro-fracking'* (Shepard, 2012).

The OWS 'We are the 99%' slogan was described as *'a national shorthand for income disparity'* and *'... a simple and statistically undeniable socio-economic ratio and transferred it directly into a political slogan'* which *'... stood out against a long US tradition of single-issue-movements and identity politics'* (Rehmann, 2013).

OWS participants have since developed other projects. Occupy Sandy was formed as Hurricane Sandy battered New York City and New Jersey in October 2012. Occupy Wall Street participants established a network of hurricane relief including donation centres, mutual aid hubs, repaired houses damaged by the flooding and generated $1.3m (£783,000) in donations. Strike Debt! is a nationwide movement of debt resistors fighting for economic justice and democratic freedom. Occupy groups in other us cities have taken action against foreclosures and prevented evictions.

**Greater Toronto Workers Assembly**

The Greater Toronto Workers Assembly (GTWA), in Canada operates through a general assembly, an elected coordinating committee plus political development and education, public sector campaign, international solidarity, feminist action, cultural and free and accessible transit campaign committees. It has a flying squad committee of labour and community activists that organises support for strikes, lockouts and demonstrations. The GTWA's political and educational work has been vitally important in supporting action and developing a solidarity platform of demands:

> *'Many unions are pursuing short-term strategies that fend off or minimize the impact of the crisis on their own members, but fail to address its underlying causes, challenge the inequalities it is reinforcing, and build the necessary alliances with the unemployed and the thousands of people living on various forms of social assistance'* (http://www.workersassembly.ca).

**Public Service Alliances in the UK**

Barnet Public Service Alliance (BAPS) is a coalition of residents, campaign groups and trade unions campaigning for high quality services in the London Borough of Barnet. Launched in September 2010, with over 200 people attending, it initially focused opposition to the council's One Barnet mass outsourcing plan and has since coordinated action against a wide range of austerity measures and public policies. BAPS holds open weekly meetings, supports local campaigns, organises demonstrations and coordinates evidence and interventions at council meetings. It is a model local authority or city-wide grassroots Public Sector Alliance.

A TUC regional umbrella Northern Public Service Alliance has eleven local area coalitions in Tyne and Wear, Teesside and Cumbria to promote alternatives to public spending cuts, campaign to protect public services and public sector employment and build coalitions with public service users. They involve UNISON and Public and Commercial Service Union (PCS) branches and have focused on TUC supported industrial action, rallies, lobbies and support for national demonstrations.

**US Worker Centres and community organising**

In the last decade Worker Centres have widened local membership, created new chapters locally and in other cities, established stronger strategic alliances with trade unions and national alliances with social justice organisations. By 2012 there were 214 Centres, which have a critical role in organising, living wage advocacy and support for low wage, primarily private sector, immigrant workers. Most Centres have public, foundation and trade union funding.

Make the Road New York is the largest participatory immigrant organisation with 11,000 members rooted in Latino working class communities and engaged in workplace justice campaigns, action against uncontrolled rent increases and safe schools. It provides literacy and workforce development, legal services, access to health insurance and services to students and job seekers. New York communities for change persuaded several municipal authorities to close their accounts with JP Morgan Chase Bank and exposed the foreclosure crisis in New York.

Domestic Workers United helped found the National Domestic Workers Alliance that has thirty three affiliates in seventeen cities and a strategic alliance with national unions and the AFL-CIO; the Restaurant Opportunities Center of New York now operates from eight cities; and the National Day Laborer Organising Network has twenty-nine affiliates (Fine, 2011). The Vermont Worker Center's People's Budget Campaign seeks fundamental change in the state's budget and revenue policy.

**Peoples Assembly's**

A National People's Assembly was held in Britain in June 2013 with the objective of building a permanent coherent mass movement against austerity. The emphasis was on 'joining up' trade unions, protest groups and to help mobilise people against austerity. Local Peoples Assembly's have been held in many cities building on previously established local coalition of resistance groups. This approach contrasts with the 15M movement in Spain that originated outside of trade union and political party structures.

**Trades and central labour councils**

Many of the UK's 160 Trades Councils have been actively engaged in local cuts campaigns, while others have been unable to revive the political economy research and activism of previous decades. US Central Labour Councils have created coalitions, local economic research and work on community issues:

> *'Even amid tight public budgets, using leverage over zoning, land use decisions, tax incentives, and other mechanisms of local governance has provided an avenue for labor to take up activism in other areas that directly affect people's lives: transportation, housing, and community development'* (Dean, 2012).

**New US trade union strategy**

The American Federation of Labor and Congress of Industrial Organisations (AFL-CIO) launched an initiative in 2013 to build a broader coalition to advance a worker economic and political agenda. It invites non-union members into the Working America organisation that already has 3.2 million members not represented in workplace bargaining. Progressive groups such as worker centres, public policy organisations, community organisations, civil rights, feminist, environmental and student groups will become partners or affiliates of the AFL-CIO.

The need for radical change has been widely advocated:

> *'... unions need to link their survival to the promotion of the common good'* (McCartin, 2013)

> *'... labor needs a vision (and a program) of what a more equitable society would look like and what it takes to achieve it. This move would shift labor's strategy toward independent political action and away from legalism'* (Aronowtiz, 2011)

> *'Organised labor must provide concrete reasons for people to see it not as a special interest group for a few sheltered workers, but as a leader in crafting solutions to community problems'* (Dean, 2012).

Movement demands must be inclusive between workers and community needs; policies that affect collective resources such as progressive taxation, increased corporate taxes; and inclusive of all instead of the divisive 'hard working families' and 'middle class values' (Luce, 2012).

For example, the AFL-CIO forged a partnership with United Students Against Sweatshops (USAS) in September 2013. USAS is the

> *'... Largest youth-led campaign organization dedicated to building a student-labor movement. Its affiliated locals on over 150 campuses run locally and nationally-coordinated campaigns for corporate accountability and economic justice, working in partnership with organizations of workers. USAS campaigns expose and hold accountable corporations that exploit people who work on campuses, in communities and in the overseas factories where collegiate apparel is produced'* (AFL-CIO, 2013).

The agreement for new tactics for shared planning, strategies, and organising to strengthen each party's movements better advances the interests of both students and workers.

There are concerns about developing effective strategies to defend and revive existing trade union membership, the potential effect of diluted forms of membership, and the difficulty of relying on existing members to finance the new alliances. However, if unions don't deliver to those same members they may not take a meaningful role in the new broader alliance (Olney, 2013 and Early, 2013).

**Building political support**

The most dramatic gains were made by Greece's Syriza (Coalition of the Radical Left – Unitary Social Front) formed in 2004, which won 71 seats and 27% share of the votes in the June 2012 national election. Smaller parties such as Spain's United Left and the Union Progress and Democracy centre party and Ireland's United Left Alliance have made small gains in comparison. New parties have been formed, such as Left Unity in the UK, but have yet to contest elections. European elections in May 2014 should indicate the level of support in many countries.

## Key issues and future strategies

Austerity measures are set to continue for many more years irrespective of whether countries exit bailout programmes and/or show early signs of economic growth. Hence the assessment and debate about lessons learned must continue.

Australia has fortunately not experienced the intensity of austerity policies elsewhere. Trade unions have adopted creative forms of industrial action to minimize job losses and real wage cuts. However, comparing tactics in negotiating annual pay increases is quite different from responding to large centrally imposed pay and pension cuts. They underestimate the potential impact of neoliberal policies and austerity measures. Furthermore, internal trade union organisational reforms and workplace activism is unlikely to constitute an effective challenge to austerity and neoliberal policies. Australia's restrictive industrial action laws means that trade unions should draw on the experience of joint industrial, community and social movement action elsewhere.

### Opposing austerity and neoliberal transformation in the public sector

#### Organising

- New approaches to organising, building alliances and action strategies will require a degree of ideological and cultural change within trade unions, community and civil society organisations. This could be addressed through education, training, recruitment and practical engagement in coalitions.

- Trade union, student union and community membership models are vitally important in organising and sustaining action strategies. They provide organisational structures, resources, a degree of stability and varying degrees of democratic accountability. It should not be a competition between organisational and 'movement' models, but how they can all contribute to the same objectives and demands (for example AFL-CIO). Participants in campaigns and social movements may politically identify with organisations or movements, but not necessarily through formal membership. Traditional organisational strengths are often overstated and weaknesses covered up to maintain bureaucratic control. This may also be intended to prevent political challenge to existing relations with social democratic parties, which in many cases, now occupy the right of centre political ground. Trade unions need to build more sustainable alliances that organise and jointly campaign on the economic, social, health, environmental and social justice challenges confronting their members, families and communities.

- Young people (unemployed, students, employed, carers) should be supported so that they can be more actively engaged in struggles they deem important.

  '*... the anti-precarity networks have been able to create a vibrant political space in*

*Portugal – unfortunately this space is more virtual than concrete. These groups work very efficiently with new media: they have established a series of blogs and websites used by precarious workers to share experiences and discuss politics and have also built up good relations to the traditional media, allowing them to highlight demands and campaigns in the mainstream news. But the core group of organisers is small and has grown very little through the years, precisely because of their rootlessness.'*
*'... the movement has punched above its own weight on multiple occasions, giving many of us the illusion that we are stronger than we actually are. This is a problem as it means we neglect building rooted sustainable networks of resistance in the workplaces and communities, but rather focus on large one-off demonstrations that are not followed up with further struggle.'* (Principe, 2013).

Action against austerity saw a step change in the use of digital communications to establish movement networks, organise direct action, build support and keep those involved up to date with information, evidence and events. This unquestionably was reflected in better organised and sustainable campaigns. On the other hand, a word of warning is reflected by the Bristol & District Anti-Cuts Alliance (2013):

> *'... just because you are a 'friend' of an anti-cuts Facebook page or follow the right blogs doesn't mean you are actually doing anything or have access to political analysis.'*

**Action strategies**

- Most local and national anti-cuts campaigns were essentially defensive and rarely changed national public spending programmes. However, cuts to public sector pay and pensions, welfare benefits and public services would have taken an even larger share of austerity measures if opposition had been less forceful. Coordinated European and national demonstrations and marches were important to rally support to show the high level of opposition to austerity policies. However, they were, in part, predictable and repetitive and more European-wide coordinated local/regional action might have been more effective in organising and challenging austerity policies.

- Single-issue campaigns are increasingly rare because attacks on workers' rights and collective bargaining are usually part of the austerity agenda of budget cuts, outsourcing and privatisation. Trade unions have to ensure that organising and action strategies are, and remain, focused on the wider agenda in the workplace, community and economy.

- Privatisation has mutated and created new ways in which services and assets can be outsourced, transferred or sold to the private sector. This has a profound impact on jobs, incomes, the quality of services and the way people live their lives. Resistance and alternatives to these policies should be a key priority.

- Trade unions must be more proactive in advancing alternative policies and innovation to retain and improve in-house services. Local strategic advice, research and investigation and technical expertise is needed locally to intervene more effectively in the review, options appraisal, business case and procurement processes. This will require a re-prioritisation of objectives and resources to achieve a step change in trade union capability and capacity.

- There have been many examples of action targeted at banks and financial institutions. It is vital to maintain the demand for fundamental reform and re-regulation of the financial system. Failure to do so could lead to the return of a laissez faire approach and another financial and economic crisis sooner than would otherwise be the case.

- Corporate interests are demanding even deeper public spending cuts, workplace 'reform' and privatisation whilst ensuring corporate welfare subsidies and tax breaks are protected. US trade unions and public policy organisations have exposed the activities of the right wing American Legislative Exchange Commission (ALEC), foundations and think tanks in promoting austerity and neoliberalism. Challenging and confronting corporate interests should be an integral part of action strategies.

- The financial crisis created opportunities to accelerate the neoliberal transformation of the public sector and welfare state (Whitfield, 2013a). There was a lack of national strategies to address these policies and to provide support and resources to tackle outsourcing and the transfer of public services to social enterprises (Whitfield, 2013b). Despite UK Coalition policies since 2010 and subsequent legislation to radically restructure and privatise the NHS, a national demonstration was not held until September 2013.

- Demonstrations succeeded in increasing the profile of tax avoidance by global companies and the wealthy and the importance of tax revenue in sustaining public services and the welfare state. Although various policies and action plans have been agreed internationally, implementation is awaited and pressure must be maintained.

- The quality of service, democratic accountability and social justice should become a core part of trade union organising, campaigning and negotiating. This may require rethinking the way industrial action is planned and organised with greater emphasis given to building wider community support.

- The trade union twin-track strategy to oppose Public Private Partnerships (PPPs) nationally, but negotiate locally on individual projects, is only a viable strategy if it includes a national alliance of trade unions, community and civil society organisations. This never materialised. Involvement in the procurement process was limited to employment matters for most trade union branches'. PPPs have since become embedded in more countries and PPP markets in finance, construction, operators and consultants have expanded globally.

- The way in which infrastructure, regeneration and development projects are planned and managed should be more rigorously challenged. Intervention at an early stage of the planning and procurement processes is vital in developing trade union and community strategies, more specifically in times of austerity.

- Success in Iceland was not repeated elsewhere because the intensity and focus was much more difficult to achieve in larger countries. Nevertheless, important lessons can be drawn from the combination of political, trade union and community action.

- The UK voluntary sector is now deeply divided between organisations engaging in the outsourcing public services and those opposing this approach in principle, because of the potential weakening of advocacy. It mirrors developments in the US non-profit sector between advocacy/campaigning and service provision roles. The National Coalition for Independent Action has organised opposition to this pro-contracting approach, but further action is needed to prevent the voluntary sector adopting private sector employment practices in a race to the bottom to win contracts.

Democratic accountability, participation and transparency are vital in trade unions, community organisations and social movements, not just in government and the economy. Austerity campaigns reflect very different approaches to decision making ranging from 15M and Occupy movement assemblies to top-down decision-making in large membership organisations. This should spur the development of more participative democratic forms of decision making.

# Chapter 3
# Alternatives to Austerity: Investment, Innovation and Reconstruction

## Key findings

**The alternative economic and political strategy to Austerity should consist of:**

- Economic stimulus strategies, industrial investment and innovation, the reconstruction of the state and public services, more rapid reform of banks and financial markets, radical reduction in corporate welfare and an increase in the labour share of national income are viable and sustainable alternatives to austerity measures.

- Financial reforms, progressive taxation, a Financial Transactions Tax, increased corporate and high-earner tax rates, a big reduction in tax avoidance and a radical reduction in corporate welfare subsidies and grants would provide enormous new resources for investment and innovation. Plus, new European Union, national and local bonds could further increase investment programmes.

**Economic stimulus and investment**

- Public infrastructure investment increases growth and output, reduces the cost of production, increases productivity, improves access, enhances the quality of services, creates jobs and generates further economic activity and jobs in local and national economies.

- Public spending on infrastructure, goods and services has a much larger multiplier effect than personal and corporate tax cuts.

- European Union and national economic stimulus strategies should stimulate growth and jobs by targeting sectors such as renewable energy; the production and dissemination of knowledge and application of information and communications technology; health, welfare and caring; sustainable solutions to food, public transport, construction, energy, water and waste.

- New industrial strategies and more proactive and interventionist government agencies are needed to increase and target research and development to sustain innovation.

- Public investment in renewable energy projects and retrofitting homes and buildings could advance a clean energy economy, reduce emissions, stimulate economic growth and jobs and improve the quality of life.

- Alternative economic strategies should focus on reducing inequalities by extending and improving universal health, social care, education, childcare, social security, and access to good quality affordable housing.

- International cooperation is essential to tackle financial market reforms, tax avoidance, collective bargaining and to challenge the purpose and scope of free trade agreements currently being negotiated.

**Reconstructing the state and public services**

- The closure of the pathways to privatisation would have an immediate effect at relatively low cost. Measures should include in-house Service Innovation and Improvement Plans; a ban on transfers of public services to trading companies or social enterprises; an end to public sector market-making activities; phasing out vouchers, direct payments, personal budgets and public sector involvement in the social investment market; and terminating planned Public Private Partnerships and nationalising/buying-out existing projects.

- Representative, participative, accountable and transparent government at international, national and local levels must have a vital role in an alternative economic strategy.

**Reform of the financial system**

- Debt reduction is a slow process and must take account of increasing uncertainty about economic growth, interest rates, long-term public spending pressures, the effectiveness of financial reform and costs arising from future financial crises.

- More radical and faster reform of banks, shadow banking, credit rating agencies and financial market regulatory regimes is urgently needed.

**Radical reduction in corporate welfare**

- The corporate welfare system of tax reliefs, subsidies, guarantees and regulatory concessions to business must be radically reduced and redirected to direct public investment. The corporate sector should invest a significant proportion of their cash hoardings in sustainable development projects.

- Reverse the significant decline in corporate income tax rates and the average effective tax rate.

**Increasing labour share of national income**

- Austerity policies, financialisation, welfare state retrenchment, the growing gap between average wages and productivity increases and declining union density, have led to a reduction in the labour share of national income and increasing inequality.

- The labour share of national income could be increased by a combination of increased national minimum and living wage rates, reduction of the gender pay gap, a cap on excessive financial and business sector salaries, increased trade union membership and collective bargaining, together with policies to create full employment.

- Trade unions, community and civil society organisations must be closely involved in the drawing up of alternative economic strategies to ensure they are comprehensive and fully incorporate their needs and interests.

- Staff/trade union and user/community organisation involvement in the planning, design and delivery of services, workforce development, childcare provision, equalities mainstreaming, good quality pensions and collective bargaining are essential parts of the reconstruction strategy.

- Alternative economic strategies should provide a springboard for the preparation of more detailed visions, plans and strategies for sectors, services, regions and localities that could be integrated into trade union, civil and community organisation and protest movement organising and action strategies.

## The alternative to austerity

This chapter sets out an alternative to austerity through economic stimulus, reconstruction of public services and the welfare state, faster fundamental reform of banks and financial markets, the elimination of corporate welfare and strategies to increase the labour share of national income.

### The need for an alternative

The financial crisis was caused by the failure of markets and deregulation. It was a private sector failure, not a sovereign debt crisis caused by excessive government spending. Neoliberal ideology and values, such as free trade, competition, debt-driven consumerism, tax cuts for the wealthy, deregulation and privatisation, underpinned economic policies and attitudes.

Austerity policies have led to soaring economic costs, rising unemployment, public sector job losses, cuts to wages, pensions and benefits, closures and business failures, financial crises in towns and cities, foreclosures and house price slump, damage to health, poverty and widening inequality. These are not temporary impacts, because austerity measures are being implemented for a longer period than originally intended and have long-term consequences. Furthermore there is no plan to 'restore' wages and benefits or to reverse the 'reforms' (Chapter 2).

### Short-term fiscal stimulus initiatives

Virtually all G20 countries had announced fiscal stimulus policies by March 2009. Fifteen planned to increase infrastructure investment, mainly on transportation networks between 2008-2010 (International Monetary Fund, 2009). However, most measures were temporary, short-term and subsequently replaced by austerity policies.

For example, the American Recovery and Reinvestment Act (ARRA) comprised 35% transfer payments, mainly unemployment insurance, 24% tax cuts, 22% for state and local government education and health care, and 19% for infrastructure. The ARRA contributed to GDP each year (2009-2011) and unemployment would otherwise have been up to 1.8% higher. However, the US$782bn (£471bn) programme failed to generate a strong recovery because it relied too heavily on tax cuts as a means of bolstering private spending; household wealth declined dramatically during the recession, which in turn weakened the willingness of households to increase spending; and credit markets were locked up, especially for smaller businesses (Pollin, 2012a).

The 2012 European Union Summit launched a €120bn (£98.4bn) Compact for Growth and Jobs. It comprised €10bn (£82bn) capital increase in the European Investment Bank to increase its lending capacity to €60bn (£49.2bn) over four years, the redirection of €55bn (£45bn) unspent EU Structural Funds to tackle youth unemployment and the launch of a pilot phase of Project Bonds to increase investment by €4.5bn (£3.7bn) in transport, energy and broadband projects (European Council, 2012).

The Compact was described as *'... full of hot air ... and little more than window dressing for voters and financial markets'* after French President Hollande promised voters a growth pact *'... to counteract Germany's obsession with austerity'* (Der Spiegel, 2012). A later review of progress concluded *'... a half-hearted implementation of the half-hearted EU summit decisions'* (Griffiths-Jones and Kollatz-Ahen, 2013).

These initiatives were limited to fiscal stimulus policies and could not be described as alternative economic strategies.

New objectives are needed to provide a framework for an alternative economic strategy and reconstruction of the state and public services and to replace the failed neoliberal objectives (see Table 5).

**Table 5: Reconstruction Objectives**

| Neoliberal objectives | Alternative economic strategy and reconstruction objectives |
|---|---|
| Free trade, competition & markets to allocate resources and deliver services and state control of money supply | **Economic stimulus, increased public investment, re-industrialisation and innovation policies, closure of pathways to privatisation** |
| Deregulate to create new opportunities for accumulation | **Public ownership with re-regulation of financial system and markets** |
| Deconstruct democracy to partnership between state and finance/business and consolidate corporate welfare | **Democratic governance, accountability, participation, transparency and minimal corporate welfare** |
| Reconfigure the role of the state to reduce functions and cut taxes | **Increase capacity of state to fulfill functions, strengthen welfare state and progressive taxation** |
| Reduce the cost and power of labour | **Quality employment and pensions, collective bargaining & trade union recognition** |

*'Three decades in which market liberals have pushed policies based on ideas of efficiency and claims about the efficiency of financial markets have not produced much in the way of improved economic performance, but they have led to drastic increases in inequality, particularly in the English-speaking world. Economists need to return their attention to policies that will generate a more equitable distribution of income' (Quiggin, 2012).*

The financialisation, personalisation, marketisation and privatisation of life, resources and economic and social relations must be challenged in the economy, not just in the public sector and welfare state.

# Economic stimulus and investment

This section begins with a summary of four economic strategy proposals.

## Alternative economic policy for Europe

The European Economists for an Alternative Economic Policy for Europe propose that governments should be released from a highly restrictive fiscal policy with higher levels of public spending financed by reversing the repeated tax cuts. The objective should be full employment with decent work. Government deficits should be financed through Eurobonds.

A new industrial policy would consist of a Europe-wide public investment plan for socio-ecological reconstruction to boost European demand; a drive to develop new environmentally sustainable, knowledge intensive, high skill and high wage economic activities; a reversal of privatisations and substantial public-sector support for new activities at the EU, national, regional and local level: '*... a new trend towards a different kind of "security" connected with disarmament, greater cohesion and reduced imbalances within the EU and individual countries; and the creation of a major new policy tool for an ecological transformation of Europe'* (EuroMemo Group, 2014).

Targeted sectors should include the protection of the environment and promotion of renewable energy; the production and dissemination of knowledge and application of information and communications technology; health, welfare and caring; sustainable solutions to food, mobility, construction, energy, water and waste (ibid). Funding arrangements should vary depending on the 'public' dimension as '*... public funds should go to public investment in non-market activities; public funds and long term private investment combined to fund new "strategic" market activities, such as the provision of public capital for new activities in emerging sectors; public support could stimulate financial markets to invest in private firms and non-profit organisations developing "good" market activities that could more easily repay the investment'* (Pianta, 2013).

*In all cases, the rationale for financing industrial policy cannot be reduced to the financial logic of the "return on investment". The benefits in terms of environmental quality, social welfare, greater territorial cohesion, more diffused growth at the European level have to be considered, and the costs have to be shared accordingly'* (ibid).

## New path for Europe

The European Trade Union Confederation's 'New Path for Europe' would invest an additional 2% of European Union GDP per year over a 10-year period. In the short term the plan would increase employment by 1.7m people in 2015 and by nearly 6.0m in 2019. Output in the EU-27 countries would increase by 1.6% in 2015 rising to nearly 5% per annum after five years.

Over a ten-year period the plan could increase Europe's GDP by €312bn (£256bn) and create between 7.2m-8.8m full-time jobs. It would increase tax revenue by €83bn, social security contributions by €45bn (£36.9bn) and make a €16bn (£13.1bn) saving in unemployment benefit. It would save €300bn in fossil fuel imports. The initiative could be financed though the European Investment Bank, or a new body, via increased share capital and the issue of long-term bonds to take advantage of '... *the large volumes of saving both within and outside the EU seeking secure investment opportunities'* (European Trade Union Confederation, 2013).

## Marshall plan for Europe

The Marshall Plan for Europe would focus '... *investments in sustainable power generation, in reducing energy consumption, in sustainable industries and services, in training and education, in research and development, in modern transport infrastructures, low-emission cities and municipalities'* (Confederation of German Trade Unions, 2012).

The 10-year plan would seek to eliminate the need for fuel imports in the long term and achieve large reductions in CO2 emissions in Europe. The plan proposes direct public sector investment, investment grants for companies and incentives for consumer spending. It would be financed through a new 'European Future Fund' which would issue 'new deal bonds' to attract the €27,000bn cash assets in Western Europe. Interest payments on the bonds would be funded from the planned Financial Transactions Tax.

## Plan B for UK

A new public investment agency is similarly proposed in Plan B for the UK, launched by Compass. It calls for a British Investment Bank to invest in low carbon, high unemployment sectors such as housing, transport and renewable energy (Compass,

2011). The government has since launched a Green Investment Bank '… a feeble and anaemic version of what Plan B suggested' (Reed, 2012). Plan B calls for a new round of quantitative easing to invest in Green New Deal projects *'... rather than blindly buying up government debt and other assets and hoping that some proportion of the extra cash punted out to the commercial banks gets lent out to productive businesses rather than fuelling speculation and financial intermediation'* (Reed, 2012).

Plan B called for the full separation of retail and commercial banking, mixed ownership of the banking sector with a larger role for mutual and co-op banks, and a substantial state-owned sector under democratic control. Labour market reform would include a living wage, reduced pay differentials, and enhanced industrial democracy and comprehensive affordable high-quality childcare.

Reform of the tax and benefit system would provide a basic minimum standard of living in or out of work and higher tax rates for those on high incomes (Reed, 2012). Unfortunately, the 'social investment state' proposals in Plan B do not take account of the scope of neoliberal transformation, and the implementation of proposals for a 'new state that spends better' could perversely accelerate this process (Whitfield, 2012d).

> *'... it is equally important to move beyond an economy of need, in which work is seen as a burden only undertaken under the stimuli of reward or deprivation, towards one aimed at improving the quality of work; that is intrinsically satisfying because it is creative and meaningful'* (Radice, 2012).

## Industrial investment and innovation

France established a new Bank of Public Investment in 2012 to provide financial support for small and medium-sized enterprises. The bank's €20bn (£16.4bn) capital gives it a €20bn (£16.4bn) lending capacity, €12bn (£9.8bn) for credit guarantees and similar sum for equity investment. It incorporates three existing state agencies – FSI, a strategic investment fund, the OSEO fund for small business development and the business lending arm of the Caisse des Depots et Consignations (Financial Times, 2012b).

France followed up with a re-industrialisation strategy with €3.7bn (£3.0bn) to invest in new technologies in 34 sectors ranging from robotics, renewable energy, medical biotechnologies and electrical transport. Each sector or project has a state appointed 'industrial officer' or project leader, mainly chief executives from major French companies. The strategy aims to create 475,000 jobs over ten years (Invest in France Agency, 2013 and Reuters, 2013b).

*'There is nothing in the DNA of the public sector that makes it less innovative than the private sector'* (Mazzucato, 2013). The state has played a central role in funding, supporting and development of computers (for example, Apple), the Internet,

biotechnology, green technology, pharmaceuticals, aeronautical and space industries and even in research and development in the nineteenth century.

The state should not be limited to *'... "de-risking" the private sector and correcting 'market failures"'* but should also reap returns from the risk taking. *'Reaping the returns is crucial, because the innovation cycle can thus be sustained over time (with returns from the current round funding the next round – as well as the inevitable losses along the way) and be less susceptible to political and business cycles'* (ibid).

Mazzucato (2013) recommends a large increase in research and development in national innovation agencies, more proactive interventionist approach to green technology innovation together with an increased green budget. These policies would be partly financed by the closure of enterprise zones, the termination of direct transfers to small firms, such as small business rate relief, limit research and development tax credits to actual spending on innovation, and require part of the return on investment financed by the public sector to be returned to government.

## Clean energy economy

Economic stimulus policies provide a unique opportunity to take a big step towards a clean energy economy. Government investment and regulatory frameworks in clean energy stimulates economic growth with environmental benefits. It creates more jobs, dollar for dollar, than equivalent spending on road construction, fossil fuel energy projects or tax cuts (United Nations Environment Programme Sustainable Energy Alliance, 2009).

A UK plan to reduce emissions by 80% in electricity, buildings and transport over twenty years could create one million new climate change jobs. A National Climate Service would be established by the government to employ teams of construction workers to refit homes and buildings, engineers to design and build wind farms and to plan, build and operate public transport systems (Campaign Against Climate Change, 2010).

Increased production of renewable electricity would create 425,000 jobs, refitting buildings to make them adaptable to climate change (150,000 jobs), changing transport (325,000), industry and landfill (50,000) and education (50,000). A further half-million jobs would be created in the supply and service industries, plus the new jobs will generate additional employment through increased household spending on goods and services in the local economy. The net effect would be a gain of 1.33m jobs in the economy after 20 years of the programme (ibid).

The net cost of the programme would be about £18bn per annum after taking account of higher tax and social insurance revenue from the new jobs, lower unemployment benefit costs, energy payments and public transport fares (ibid). Some UK local authorities are developing new municipal energy plants that add to the stock of district heating schemes (Hetherington, 2013).

Freiburg and Hamburg (Germany), Aarhus and Copenhagen (Denmark), Vienna (Austria) and Gothenburg (Sweden) are examples of European green cities. Bristol City Council is the first UK local authority to own a wind farm. It will generate electricity to 2,500 households, cut the city's annual carbon footprint by around 5,000 tonnes per annum generate £200,000 income (LocalGov, 2013).

In the Republic of Ireland, Tralee Town Council operates a biomass district heating scheme using woodchip from a nearby 55,000 hectares of forest and has made significant fuel bill savings. It originated in a regeneration scheme, was extended to more houses, a day care centre, library and primary school and phase two will include Kerry General Hospital and supply heat to over 7,000 people and public buildings. The Town Council maintains the district heating plant and purchases wood chip through a producer cooperative that created over 100 jobs (Sustainable Energy Authority of Ireland, 2011).

Hamburg plans to re-municipalise electricity, gas and district heating distribution grids when concessions are up for renewal in 2014 and 2016. Since 2007, 44 new local public utilities have been set up in Germany with more than 100 energy distribution network concessions now publicly operated (Hall, 2012). The planned return of water services to public provision in Berlin follows the highly successful re-municipalisation of water services in Paris in 2010.

Many municipally-owned US Public Utility Districts have provided electricity, and often water, for over a century. For example, Sacramento Municipal Utility District generates, transmits and distributes electric power to a 900 square-mile area of California. Residential electric rates were up to a third cheaper than other utilities in the state, 28% of supplies came from renewable resources and nearly 50% came from non-carbon emitting sources (Sacramento Municipal Utility District, 2013).

Although a clean energy economy will retrofit buildings and infrastructure nationally, it must take account of regional equity issues, such as differences in climate and topography and the disproportionate negative impacts in more fossil fuel dependent regions (Pollin, 2012b).

## Public ownership and provision

Governments should ensure that state owned corporations and public bodies operate to public service principles and management practice, have democratic and accountable governance and continuing training and education on the function, objectives and political economy at all levels of the organisation.

Programmes of re-municipalisation and re-nationalisation could reverse the privatisation of state owned corporations, health and social care, education, public housing, land and public buildings. They could include the termination or buyout of

Public Private Partnerships that privatised the design, build, finance and operation of eleven types of public infrastructure (Whitfield, 2010).

Public infrastructure investment is vital for the economy and to improve quality of life. Improving public transport (rail, tram and bus); primary healthcare facilities; public housing; low carbon construction, renewable energy, renovating buildings; integrated multi-use facilities for education, sport and leisure, library, childcare and other community services should be prioritised. Production and supply chains, for example, trains and rolling stock, ICT and other equipment, furniture, goods and services, should be integrated with industrial policies, economic development and employment strategies. A public design initiative would set new standards for the design and planning of public buildings and infrastructure (Whitfield, 2012b).

Austerity policies have highlighted the need for governments to maximise control over natural resources, such as oil and gas reserves and forests. Privatisation also means the potential loss of significant longer-term tax revenue.

## Welfare state tackling inequalities

Alternative economic strategies should focus on reducing inequalities, particularly since women, and disabled and elderly women and men in particular, have borne the brunt of austerity measures and widened inequalities. Strategies need to address income and wealth inequality, discrimination in access to services, the restoration/strengthening of legal rights and taxation inequalities.

The welfare state has a vital role in addressing risk and uncertainty through social insurance, income redistribution, public goods and the provision of basic needs. 'Collective risk management through the welfare state helps to stabilize the aggregate economy' (Quiggin, 2012).

The welfare state must be strengthened with investment targeted to extend and improve:

- Universal health and social care, education and training;
- Universal childcare for all preschool children;
- Universal social security through state and occupational pensions with a responsive benefits system to protect against unemployment and other unforeseen circumstances;
- Access to good quality affordable housing; and
- Public delivery of public goods.

The comprehensive case for universalism is cogently set out in Danson et al (2012).

In addition to targeting inequalities through universal welfare provision, more progressive taxation methods have a vital role to play. The EU has favoured indirect taxation on goods and services, but this '... *tends to compound income inequalities: it has a regressive, rather than progressive, effect, especially if basic goods are not exempted, because poorer families spend a higher proportion of their household income on consumption and are able to save less. A more effective, long-term solution, to both fiscal modernisation and to social justice, is the establishment of an efficient and fair system of progressive direct taxation, in which the rate of taxation rises in proportion to the level of income. In this area of direct taxation, the EU and its member states have arguably been very poor examples of both principle and practice'* (EuroMemo Group, 2012).

Governments should carefully monitor prices, income/loan ratios and the buy-to-let sector in housing markets and consider effective measures, such as increased interest rates and/or control of planning permissions, to prevent further housing and property bubbles, foreclosures, evictions and crash of the construction sector.

## The benefits of public investment

There is an enormous amount of economic evidence that public investment has a significant positive effect on private sector productivity – hence growth in average living standards – and increases both output and jobs (Bivens, 2012). Analysis of government purchase multipliers for a large number of OECD countries concluded '... *that fiscal policy activism may indeed be effective at stimulating output during a deep recession, and that the potential negative side effects of fiscal stimulus, such as increased inflation, are also less likely under these circumstances.'* A one billion dollar increase in US government spending is estimated to create approximately 44,000 jobs (Auerbach and Gorodnichenko, 2011).

Despite different models, evidence, assumptions, economic conditions and time periods there is broad consensus on the output multipliers for different types of expenditure. For example, multipliers range from 0.5 to 2.5 for purchases of goods and services by the Federal Government under the ARRA, 0.4 to 2.2 for infrastructure and 0.1 to 0.6 for a one-year tax cut for higher income people (Congressional Budget Office, 2012).

A guide to specific spending measures is provided by Zandi (2010). A US$1.00 (£0.60) increase in US infrastructure spending is estimated to result in US$1.57 (£0.95) change in real GDP one-year after the spending actually occurs – significantly larger than the multiplier effect of personal and corporate tax cuts – see Table 6.

## International co-operation

The European Trade Union Confederation (ETUC) called for increased European co-operation on tax avoidance, evasion and tax havens through comprehensive information

**Table 6: Different effect of spending increases and tax cuts**

| Multiplier effect<br>One-year $ change in real GDP per $ increase in spending or reduction in Federal tax revenue | |
|---|---|
| **Spending Increases** | |
| Temporarily Increase Food Stamps | 1.74 |
| Extend Unemployment Insurance Benefits | 1.61 |
| Increase Infrastructure Spending | 1.57 |
| Issue General Aid to State Governments | 1.41 |
| **Tax Cuts** | |
| Non-refundable Lump-Sum Tax Rebate | 1.01 |
| Refundable Lump-Sum Tax Rebate | 1.22 |
| Temporary Tax Cuts | |
| Payroll Tax Holiday | 1.24 |
| Across the Board Tax Cut | 1.02 |
| Accelerated Depreciation | 0.25 |
| Permanent Tax Cuts | |
| Extend Alternative Minimum Tax Patch | 0.51 |
| Make Bush Income Tax Cuts Permanent | 0.32 |
| Make Dividend and Capital Gains Tax Cuts Permanent | 0.37 |
| Cut Corporate Tax Rate | 0.32 |

*Source: Zandi, M., Moody's Analytics (2010)*

sharing and cooperation between national tax authorities and harmonisation of the corporate tax base. Greater cooperation on financial market reform is needed to promote long-term quality public services. The ETUC called for social partners to strengthen social dialogue, collective bargaining and worker participation, particularly in relation to the economic governance process at national and EU level, plus education and training and labour market reform. European social standards should be strengthened to fight precarious jobs and promote decent, quality jobs (ETUC, 2013).

Cooperation is needed to challenge the free trade agreements currently being negotiated – the Transatlantic Trade and Investment Partnership (TTIP) Trans-Pacific Partnership (TPP) and the Canadian Canada-European Union Comprehensive Economic and Trade Agreement (CETA) – to remove or re-write draft clauses on investor privileges, market competition, undermining of standards and rights, compensation and the power shift to corporations (Corporate Europe Observatory, 2013).

An EU alliance of over 50 civil society organisations launched an Alternative Trade Mandate in late 2013 demanding a paradigm shift in EU trade and investment policy. Twelve principles range from food production, jobs and labour rights, climate change, public procurement and democratising the initiation, to negotiation and finalisation of trade and investment agreements (Alternative Trade Mandate, 2013).

## Basic principles

Alternative economic strategies need a framework of principles to prevent policy drift and implementation diversion or failure – see Table 7.

**Table 7: Public sector principles**

| Public sector principles |
|---|
| • Democratic accountability, participation and transparency with user/employee involvement in the planning, design, delivery and policy-making processes.<br>• Social justice to eliminate discrimination and to eliminate or mitigate adverse impacts and inequalities.<br>• Good quality integrated, responsive and flexible services that meet social and community needs.<br>• Solidarity and collective responsibility through universal provision for health, education, welfare, transport and the environment.<br>• Sustainable development to take account of economic production and supply chains and conserve natural resources.<br>• Climate change policies to reduce emissions, prioritise renewable energy, retrofit homes and infrastructure.<br>• Quality employment with good terms and conditions, pensions, equalities and diversity, training and the right to organise.<br>• Evidence-based policy making with economic, social, health, equalities and environmental impact assessment and cost benefit analysis.<br>• Public goods, infrastructure and services should be designed, financed and delivered by skilled in-house staff. |

# Reconstructing the state and public services

The benefits of economic stimulus and financial reforms will be limited, and could ultimately be eroded, if national and transnational companies gain increasing power through public sector contracting, marketisation and privatisation of the welfare state. 'Business as usual' will inevitably drive down service and labour standards, further weaken the role of trade unions in the economy, with drastic economic and social consequences.

The core functions of the state must be strengthened – they include democratic governance and civil society; national and international responsibilities; human needs and development; economic and fiscal management; and the regulation of markets, firms and organisations.

## Closing the pathways to privatisation

Neoliberal transformation of public services, particularly in the UK, has created pathways to financialise, personalise and marketise services. They were designed to accelerate the mutation of privatisation to enable core services to be sliced and diced into contracts, transfer assets to trading companies, trusts, social enterprises or voluntary organisations and to impose individual choice mechanisms in marketised services (Whitfield 2012b and 2012c). It is vital to close these pathways to privatisation, to de-commodify services, to improve in-house provision and replace neoliberal public management.

A series of measures to close the pathways to privatisation would have an immediate effect at relatively low cost.

1. Abolish commissioning and re-integrate client and service provision functions with a commitment to in-house provision, would rapidly stem the flow of outsourcing contracts and PPPs. Rigorous monitoring and evaluation of current contracts could lead to terminations and/or buy-outs.

2. Service Reviews and Service Innovation & Improvement Plans should be required in all services with automatic involvement of staff/trade unions and service users/community organisations.

3. Full options appraisals and business cases undertaken before procurement (with in-house options and bids if it proceeds).

4. Terminate the transfer of public services to arm's length trading companies, trusts and social enterprises. The transfer of public services to social enterprises, mutuals or cooperatives is privatisation, irrespective of the ownership model, staff and user engagement, democratic structures and community support. Resources should be redirected to create social enterprises in the private sector (Whitfield, 2013b).

5. Public sector market-making, corporate subsidies and other commercialisation activities should cease, with resources redirected to innovation, improvement and the creation of choice within in-house provision.

6. Vouchers, direct payments and personal budgets should be rapidly phased out for all but the high-dependency social care users for whom they were originally designed. Charges for 'additional' services in health, social care and education should be stopped immediately.

7. Public sector involvement in the social investment market with venture capitalists, social bonds and payment by results should cease. Innovation within the public sector could achieve the same objectives with greater public benefit.

8. Terminate planned infrastructure Public Private Partnerships and buyout or terminate operational projects. The risks, costs and benefits of economic development, housing and regeneration partnerships should be re-assessed.

9. A Living Wage introduced in all sectors together with reduced pay differentials, defined benefit pensions safeguarded, affordable childcare and trade union recognition and collective bargaining rights.

10. Contractor and consultant bids must be rigorously assessed to determine quality standards and economic, social, environmental and equality impacts and the 'whole contract price' and community cost.

Public bodies will face strident opposition from corporate and financial interests, business and trade bodies and right-wing policy organisations that will attempt to undermine and challenge their legality. Contractors such as Veolia, IBM and Serco are almost certain to react negatively when the flow of public sector contracts starts to decline. 'Private good, public bad' has become embedded in public discourse and must be constantly challenged.

These measures need to be embedded through fundamental long-term changes, such as stronger regulatory frameworks and new public service management which centres on democratisation and participation, public planning, new innovation and improvement strategies and flatter accountable organisational structures.

## Public sector innovation

Public sector principles and values provide a framework to develop public sector innovation (see Table 7). New methods of service delivery would require changes to working methods, new equipment and/or digitisation, staff redeployment and/or retraining and the development of options/choices within public provision. New and expanded services would address unmet needs or respond to market failures.

Organisational innovation might include flatter management structures and team working or the formation of new sections/teams to undertake specific tasks. Democratic innovation would widen involvement in the policy making process or strengthen scrutiny and review by seeking written and verbal evidence from community organisations and trade unions.

Financial innovation could pool budgets, increase income generation and find new ways to raise public finance, such as bonds. Access innovation could address inequalities in service design and delivery. Workforce development innovation could range from new training and learning programmes to cross cutting service and boundary skills.

Service user and employee involvement, accountability, transparency, dialogue and negotiation are essential to build in-house capability, so that innovative ideas are part of a continuous development process in community needs analysis, service reviews and service improvement and innovation plans.

The priority must be to embed public enterprise and innovation at all levels of government. The ideology must be challenged that innovation and 'entrepreneurialism' only has value when private and third sector organisations seek to hive off functions and services to create 'mixed markets' and thus effectively dismantle the public sector and welfare state.

## Democratic governance, accountability, participation and transparency

Representative, participative, democratically accountable and transparent government at national, regional and local levels must have a vital role in reconstruction. Improved integration of functions and services, real innovation and aligning services to meet social need are direct outcomes of participative and accountable governance.

Social justice strategies should seek to eliminate discrimination and to eliminate or mitigate adverse impacts and inequalities; quality integrated services of a good standard, responsive and flexible that meet social and community needs through in-house provision; universal provision available for all unless specifically targeted; sustainable development to take account of global, national and local economic impact, production and supply chains, and to conserve natural resources.

## Quality employment and collective bargaining

Staff/trade union and user/community organisation involvement in the planning, design and delivery benefits the quality of services, jobs, innovation and the effectiveness of services. A large volume of studies has found a direct correlation between the quality of employment and the quality of service in public services and service industries. For example, job satisfaction has a significant impact on service quality and, ultimately, on organisational effectiveness in a service organisation (Snipes et al, 2005); linking employee satisfaction to customer satisfaction and perceived service quality (Brown and Lam, 2008); sustaining good working conditions for nurses is crucial to increase retention, enhance performance and productivity and promote safe nursing care (Almalki, 2012).

A direct and positive relationship was found between employee satisfaction and the quality of hospital patient experience (Peltier et al, 2009). Higher employee engagement levels improved the quality of care and increased patient satisfaction, increased productivity, improved relationships with management, reduced job stress, increased employee satisfaction and increased retention; and lowered employee recruitment, retention and training costs and possibly lower costs in the delivery of patient care.

Workforce development, childcare provision, equalities mainstreaming, good quality pensions, trade union representation, collective bargaining and facility time together with service and workplace democracy are an essential part of the reconstruction strategy.

## Public finance and fiscal crisis of cities

Governments must have the resources and ability to fund, plan, provide and regulate for the medium and long term, taking account of generational interests, innovation and transformation of the economy, redistribution, and the need to legislate and enforce regulations, protect rights, advance a social justice agenda and protect the environment. For example, a series of UK tax measures could provide £85.2bn revenue annually by reducing tax avoidance, a Financial Transaction Tax, restoring corporation tax to 28%, scrapping higher rate pension tax relief and a series of other measures (Compass, 2013).

*'Tax systems around the world have become steadily less progressive since the early 1980s. They now rely more on indirect taxes, which are generally less progressive than direct taxes, and within the latter, the progressivity of the personal income tax has declined, reflecting most notably steep cuts in top marginal tax rates'* (IMF, 2013c).

Progressive direct taxation, in which the percentage marginal tax rate increases as income rises, has an important role in promoting social justice. The breadth of the tax base is equally important. However, the move towards reduced corporate and personal income tax rates, whilst increasing taxes on goods and services, is regressive. A user-pays taxation model will prove much more expensive than public provision through general taxation. It is inequitable, regressive and significantly reduces collective provision and hastens the demise of public services and the welfare state.

A new EU investment programme, the Investment-led Recovery and Convergence Programme, co-financed by bonds issued jointly by the European Investment Bank (EIB) and the European Investment Fund (EIF), would invest in health, education, urban renewal and green technology and power generation (Varoufakis et al, 2013). Borrowing should be 'europeanised' and not count towards national debt – the EIB has issued bonds since 1998 without national guarantees. The authors also propose a Limited Debt Conversion Programme in which the European Central Bank would offer member-states the opportunity of a debt conversion for their Maastricht Compliant Debt (up to 60% of GDP) and an Emergency Social Solidarity Programme to guarantee access to nutrition (based on the US food stamp programme) and basic energy needs (ibid).

It is vital that local and regional public bodies, collectively and/or individually, are able to finance investment to complement EU and national programmes. Municipal bond agencies have been established in Sweden and Finland and an agency one is being developed in the UK by the Local Government Association after the Coalition government suddenly hiked Public Works Loans Board (the main source of local authority borrowing) interest rates in October 2010 (Local Government Association, 2013).

The fiscal crisis confronting many cities, particularly in the US, urgently require government action and support. The solution cannot be punitive and cannot be left to the same market forces that had a major role in creating the problem and to the narrow exploitative interests of vulture funds. Detroiters Resisting Emergency Management have demanded the termination and repayment of interest rate swaps with Wall Street banks and repayment; mandatory collection of local income tax; increased state-wide revenue sharing; cancellation of corporate tax relief in economic incentive programmes; and comprehensive city and neighbourhood economic development plans (http://www.d-rem.org). Despite claims to the contrary, Detroit's public pension funds are well funded by national standards (Long, 2013a).

Fiscal challenges are expected to continue for many more years (Pew Charitable Trusts, 2013) and whilst increasing sales and income tax revenue is important, more fundamental action is needed, for example, to address continued de-industrialisation, city planning and economic development and the continued fragmentation of local government by the privatisation of public education.

## Debt reduction and restructuring

Additional publicly financed investment may increase public debt in the short-term, but it will create economic benefits that will ultimately reduce national debt in the long-term. It is vital to challenge the demands of right wing deficit hawks for governments to adopt a rapid debt reduction strategy. It is important to reduce public debt, '… although it will inevitably be a slow process' (IMF, 2013c).

The European Fiscal Pact requires member states to impose a binding limit on their structural deficits, with strict rules governing any breaches, subject to sanctions imposed by the Eurozone authorities. Radice argues that the structural deficit *'... is meaningless as a policy target, since it is impossible to measure objectively; while politically, it reinforces the depoliticisation of economic policy, under which technical experts replace elected governments in managing the national economy'* (Radice, 2014).

The average public debt ratio in advanced economies is expected to stabilize in 2013–14 at slightly below 110% of GDP, 35 percentage points above its 2007 level. *'Simulations show that maintaining the overall budget at a level consistent with the IMF staff's medium-term advice would bring the average debt ratio to about 70 percent of GDP by 2030, although in a few countries it would remain above 80 percent'* (IMF, 2013d).

Debt reduction must take account of increasing uncertainty about economic growth rates, interest rates, and long-term public spending pressures.

Faster growth is an important route to reduce debt. *'... a country with a debt ratio of 100 percent of GDP could reduce its debt by 30 percent of GDP in 10 years with one additional percentage point of potential growth. This could eventually give rise to a virtuous circle in which lower debt levels would raise potential growth, further facilitating debt reduction'* (ibid). Progressive direct taxation could also help to reduce debt. High inflation would erode the real value of the debt, but would have economic and social costs.

Debt restructuring is another option. The 2012 Greek debt restructuring led to a €100bn (£82bn) transfer from private creditors to Greece, corresponding to 50% of GDP in 2012. Although *'... the Greek debt restructuring approach can be useful in specific cases, but it falls far short of providing a template that could be a permanent fixture of the European financial architecture'* (Zettelmeyer et al, 2013).

Iceland has launched a €900m (£738m) mortgage debt relief programme with a maximum limit of €24,000 (£19,672) for 100,000 households over a four-year period. In addition, employees will be able to redirect a supplementary pension, usually 2%-6% of wages, to pay off mortgages for a three-year period, free of tax (News of Iceland, 2013). The government estimates that mortgage holders who benefit from principal reduction and tax exemptions could reduce their mortgage principal by up to 20% by 2017 (Fitch Ratings, 2013). They believed Iceland had *'... little fiscal space for new measures and that across-the-board measures are costly and may not provide sufficient relief to households in most distress'* (IMF, 2013e). The programme *'... appears fiscally neutral'* (Fitch Ratings, 2013).

The debt relief programme will be funded by a levy on Iceland's failed banks (debts now held by hedge funds) and the three new banks, which acquired their loan portfolios priced at a value that took account of need for write-downs (see Chapter 1). The previous government had introduced a moratorium on foreclosures, rescheduled payments, restructured debt and wrote-down mortgages to 110% of household assets for the most indebted households (IMF, 2013f).

The International Citizen Audit Network is supporting Citizen Debt Audits in several countries to analyse the origin, composition, management and impact of public debt to identify illegitimate debt under the banner of 'We don't owe! We won't pay!'

## Reform of the financial system

The reform of financial markets and institutions is essential to ensure alternative policies are effective and sustainable. Although some financial reforms have been implemented, much remains to be achieved five years after the crash.

The European Stability Mechanism (ESM) was established by Eurozone member states in 2012 to fund future financial crises and bailouts, replacing the temporary European Financial Stability Facility, and can lend up to €500bn (£410bn). The ESM raises funds by issuing short-term securities and long-term debt. It provided €41.3bn (£33.8bn) in 2012-2013 to the Spanish government to recapitalise the banking sector and €4.5bn (£3.7bn) to Cypress to recapitalise and restructure the two largest banks (http://www.esm.europa.eu).

### Regulation and reform of banks

New global banking regulations (Basel III or Third Basel Accord) are being phased in between 2013-2018 that require banks to be more resilient to financial shocks, improve risk management, governance and transparency. Banks are required to increase capital reserves to 3%-7% of risk-weighted assets. The regulations are also intended to significantly reduce off-balance sheet financing, one of the causes of the financial crisis.

Banks buy and sell stocks, bonds and other securities on behalf of clients. New 'Volcker' rules take effect in April 2014 and will limit their ability to trade their own cash, restrict investment in high-risk hedge and private equity funds and impose compliance obligations.

Questions remain about the effectiveness of these regulations. There are concerns about how banks define assets, measure the risk of losses, determine what is off-balance sheet gross or net and the potential for gaming capital requirements. Much depends on how the regulators interpret and enforce the regulations (Wall Street Journal, 2013d and Brunsden, 2013). The complexity of the new regulations – Basel III was 616 pages and the Volcker rules over 900 pages – led Andrew Haldane, Bank of England to conclude *'... we moved from what was effectively a regulatory framework to what has become a self-regulatory framework – of banks, give or take, marking their own exams'* (Zhong, 2013).

The risk of taxpayers funding further bank bailouts led to Eurozone finance ministers agreeing the terms for a 17-member single currency banking union in December 2013. A Single Resolution Mechanism will provide a centralised system for winding down failing banks. An industry levy will create a €55bn (£45bn) fund by 2026 with a network of national resolution funds in the transitional period (Financial Times, 2013b). Germany opposed taxpayer funded Eurozone bailouts. *'It means there will be no additional taxpayer-funded eurozone safety net for the next decade, leaving any bank's home state largely to foot the bill if its collapse overwhelms the embryonic resources of the banking union system'* (Barker and Spiegel, 2013).

> *'... we need a new culture of a "will to supervise" in the financial oversight system' ... First, the supervisory bodies need to be given further-reaching rights to intervene in the banks (e.g. to scrutinise business models); second, they must make effective use of these rights to intervene; third, they must have enough staff of the right quality; and fourth, they must be obliged to inform the government, the parliament and the public early on about any signs of gaps in their supervisory powers, and to ask for this to be remedied' (Troost and Hersel, 2012).*

## Shadow banking

The shadow banking system consists of non-bank financial institutions and activities outside the regular banking system. It includes hedge funds, money market funds, special purpose vehicles and structured investment vehicles. Investment banks may conduct much of their business in the shadow banking system, although they are not shadow banking institutions themselves. The sector grew globally by 8.1% or $5tn (£3tn) in 2012 to reach $71.2tn (£42.9tn), which represents 24% of total global financial assets (Financial Stability Board, 2013a). Real estate investment trusts and funds (+30%), other investment funds (+16%) and hedge funds (+11%) were the fastest growing shadow banking sectors in 2012.

The complex task of mapping the web of transnational connections between funds and identifying systemic risks continues. In September 2013 the European Commission published a roadmap to regulate the shadow banking sector and draft regulations for money market funds. It stipulates funds should hold a cash buffer (3% of their assets), when they guarantee constant value per share, hold financial instruments that can be converted into cash daily (10% of their assets) or weekly (an additional 20% of their assets), and have better risk assessments systems of their assets and their clients (European Commission, 2013b).

A number of critical issues remain, including the strategy to mitigate spill-over effects between shadow banking and the regular banking system, transparency, how to disentangle banking from shadow banking, and '*... the pivotal role of Luxembourg, the Netherlands and Ireland in shadow banking activities since these countries are in practice offshore centers where capital is routed between shadow banking entities'* is absent from the roadmap (SOMO, 2013). The City of London has an even more pivotal role as the leading centre for transacting cross-border capital flows.

Both the EU and US strengthened regulation of hedge and private equity funds. The EU's short selling (speculative sale of securities not owned by seller and repurchase at lower price) transparency regulations, effective from 1 November 2012, had '*... mixed effects on liquidity and a slight decrease in price discovery'* (European Securities and Markets Authority, 2013).

The G20 Pittsburgh summit agreed to reduce systemic risk, improve transparency, support financial stability and combat market abuse in derivatives markets (financial contracts). A comparison of US and EU regulations found that they led to broadly similar regulatory outcomes in 15 aspects of trading (Deloitte, 2013).

The UK is challenging the legality of the ESMA powers and the Financial Transactions Tax and has sued the European Central Bank claiming its policies push the clearing of some derivatives away from the City of London and into the euro area.

The planned EU-US Transatlantic Trade and Investment Partnership has already raised disagreements over draft clauses on financial market liberalisation: '*... everything that has been achieved in recent years in the area of financial market regulation could be endangered by the inclusion of financial services in the agreement'* (World Economy, Ecology and Development, 2013).

## Credit rating agencies

Three entrenched Credit Ratings Agencies (CRA), Standard & Poor's, Moody's, and Fitch rate 96% of the world's bonds. Ratings agencies are US private companies with an 'issuer pays' business model, with financial institutions and banks paying the charges for ratings, not investors. They validated the transformation of subprime mortgages into triple A-rated securities, a gross miscalculation and a prime cause of the financial crisis.

Reform has been very slow despite CRAs being heavily criticised. The Financial Stability Board (Bank of International Settlements), responsible for international coordination of national financial authorities and implementation of effective regulatory policies, established a roadmap for reducing reliance on CRA ratings (Financial Stability Board, 2013b and G20, 2013). However, proposals to establish a European public sector ratings agency, break the oligopoly by supporting new entrants to increase competition and other proposals are still under discussion.

There is a strong case for significantly restricting the activities of credit agencies. '... *the false incentives deriving from the fact that the agencies are paid for their supposedly 'objective rating' by the very people they are rating must be ended'* (Troost and Hersel, 2012). Banks could develop capacity to self-assess loans and projects.

## Financial transactions tax

Eleven European countries, including Germany and France, are pressing ahead with a European Commission proposal for a Financial Transaction Tax (FTT) after other countries opposed the move. It will impose a 0.1% levy on stock, bond and 0.01% on derivative transactions between financial institutions if at least one party is located in the European Union. It could raise between €30bn-€35bn (£24.6bn-£28.7bn) annually after allowing for a reduction in trading volumes after its introduction (European Commission, 2013c). The UK, US and the financial institutions strongly oppose the tax.

## Tax avoidance/evasion reform

The European shadow economy results in an estimated tax revenue loss of €864bn (£708bn) per annum, nearly 20% of total economic activity, plus a further €150bn (£123bn) per annum loss through tax avoidance (Murphy, 2012).

US income tax evasion was estimated at US$500bn (£301bn) per annum in 2008 (Celuba and Feige, 2011). Canada's 'underground' economy was estimated to be C$35bn (£18.9bn) in 2009, equivalent to 2.3% of GDP (Canada Revenue Agency, 2012). However, another analysis estimated lost tax revenue from the underground economy to be significantly higher at US$79.6bn (£47.9bn) per annum, with a further C$81bn (£43.8bn) in tax evasion (Tax Justice Network, 2011).

Tax evasion in Europe and North America totals about €1,600bn (£1,311bn) annually. If a good proportion of this revenue were collected it would transform public finance in the respective countries. Yet several governments have systematically cut tax collection budgets and staffing levels. For example, over C$250m (£135m) was cut from the Canadian Revenue Agency's budget up to 2015-2016 (National Post, 2013).

Political pressures led the G8 and G20 group of world leaders to ask the Organisation for Economic Co-operation and Development (OECD) to develop an Action Plan on corporate tax avoidance. The mandate, stated in the Tax Annex of the St Petersburg Declaration issued by the G20 Summit in September 2013 is to reform international tax rules to ensure that multinationals are tax *'where economic activities take place and value is created'*. However, the Tax Justice Network has criticised the approach adopted in the OECD's Action Plan as *'... a path strewn with obstacles, and leading ultimately in the wrong direction'* *because it tries* *'... to tax transnational corporations (TNCs) as if they were loose collections of separate entities operating independently in each country. This is a system built on a fiction: the OECD knows as well as anyone that these firms are not bunches of separate entities – but unified firms under central direction'* (Tax Justice Network, 2013a).

The *'... alternative is to take a Unitary approach to taxing multinational firms. This involves taking a multinational's total global profits and apportioning them out between the states where it does business according to its genuine economic presence in each country'* (Tax Justice Network, 2013b). This would require a combined and country-by-country report to each tax authority, apportioning profits to different jurisdictions and a procedure to resolve disagreements and conflicts (ibid).

## Value Added Tax gap

The Value Added Tax (VAT) Gap increased significantly in many member countries since 2008 as a result of the economic crisis – see Figure 15. The gap is related to non-compliance under national tax rules and was €193bn (£158bn), or 1.5% of GDP for the 26 Member States in 2011 or 18% of the theoretical VAT (European Commission, 2013d).

Italy (€36bn-£29.5bn), France (€32bn-£26.2bn), Germany (€26.9bn-£22.0bn) and the UK (€19bn-£15.6bn) contributed over half of the total VAT Gap in quantitative terms, being the largest EU economies. A reduction in the VAT gap could provide states with significant additional resources.

**Figure 15: European Union 26 countries VAT gap (per cent of GDP)**

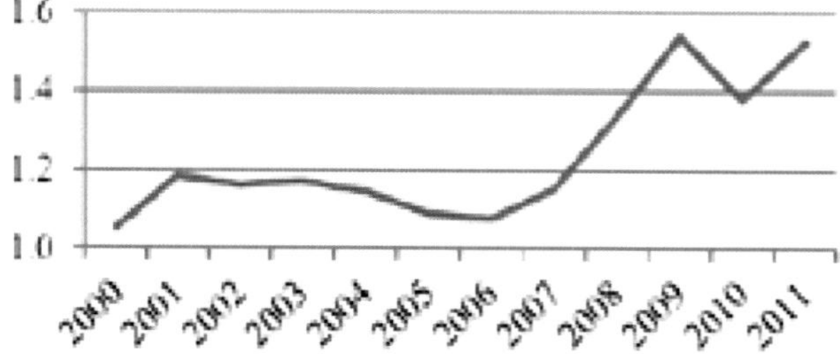


*Source: European Commission, 2013c*

## Radical reduction in corporate welfare

The corporate welfare system of tax reliefs, subsidies, guarantees and regulatory concessions to business must be radically reduced and redirected to direct public investment. For example, capital grants to business, low-wage subsidies, training and research grants, trade marketing and advice, tax subsidies such as capital allowances and various types of credits total over £100bn per annum (excluding financial market and bank support, tax avoidance and evasion) in the UK alone (Farnsworth, 2014).

Outsourcing, PPPs and privatisation lead to a contract culture and 'regulatory capture', when regulators are aligned to business interests as a result of lobbying, political pressure and ideological sympathy, and consequently prioritise and protect business interests. This 'protection' often includes refusing to identify the contractors responsible for poor performance (Whitfield, 2012a).

## Reversing corporate tax cuts

Corporate income tax rates and the average effective taxation have been significantly reduced in most European countries in the last decade – see Figure 16. The average EU-27 corporate tax rate fell from 35.3% in 1995 to 23.2% by 2013, a 12.2% difference (Eurostat, 2013d). The Effective Average Tax Rate, the percentage tax rate companies actually pay, had fallen to 20.9% in 2012. The fall in tax revenue is an inevitable consequence of states following the 'competitiveness agenda'. The tax rate for US firms operating in Ireland was 2.2% in 2011 (Stewart, 2014).

Corporate tax rates in Canada declined from 40.5% to 26.1% between 2010 and 2013 (includes Provincial tax rate). The US rate remained at 35% in the same period, excluding State taxes. However, the US Effective Average Tax Rate is significantly lower at 12.6% of worldwide income (Government Accountability Office, 20136). *'Even when foreign, state, and local corporate income taxes are included in the numerator, for tax year 2010, profitable Schedule M-3 filers actually paid income taxes amounting to 16.9 per cent of their reported worldwide income'* (ibid). Nearly 55% of all large US-controlled corporations reported no federal tax liability in at least one year between 1998 and 2005 (Government Accountability Office, 2008).

There is significant scope to increase corporate income tax rates, the average effective tax rate and to reduce harmful economic development competition between states and regions.

## Re-investing corporate cash hoardings

Capital investment by the private sector would create jobs, generate supply chain activity, stimulate demand and increase tax revenue. However, non-financial companies have been hoarding cash since the beginning of the financial crisis.

The total deposits of non-financial companies in the Euro Area increased to €1,763bn

**Figure 16: Corporate income tax rates and average effective taxation indicators, EU27 1995-2012 (5)**

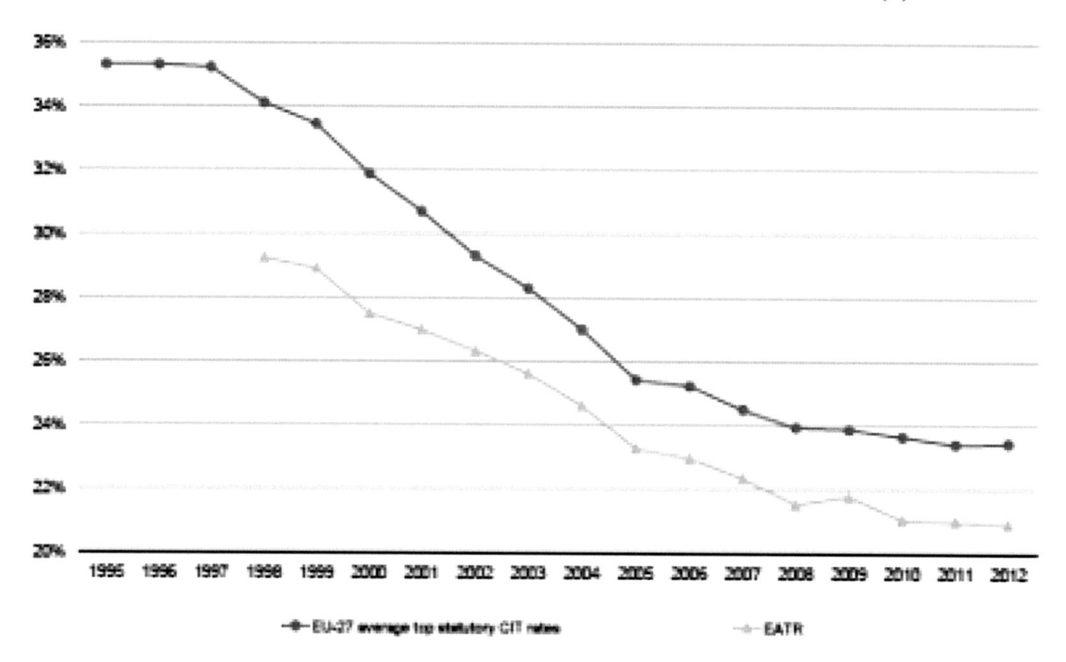


*Source: Taxation Trends in the European Union, Eurostat, 2013*

(£1,445bn) in July 2013, a 23.5% rise since January 2008. The UK rise was a staggering 455% to £419bn between the end of 2008 to July 2013 (Burke, 2013). The cash hoard of the one thousand largest US companies rose to $1,482bn (£893bn) by July 2013, an 81% since 2006. In Canada *'... because corporations are taking in so much more than they are spending, liquid cash assets in the non-financial corporate sector continue to swell, and now total almost [C]$600 billion [£324bn]'* (Stanford, 2013)

The declining proportion of profits directed to investment is revealed in the fall in the investment ratio. The Euro Area ratio fell from 53.2% in 2008 to 47.1% in 2012 with an even bigger decline in the UK from 53% in 2008 down to 42.9% in 2012 (Burke, 2013). Corporate tax rates have been cut over the same period on the assumption that they would encourage increased business investment, but precisely the opposite has occurred.

Four stark facts are evident. Firstly, corporate welfare subsidies and grants have continued to increase. Secondly, corporate cash hoarding in Europe and the US has soared. Thirdly, governments have dramatically cut corporate tax rates and/or effective average tax rates, resulting in ever decreasing corporate sector tax obligations. Finally, most cash hoards are placed in banks or the shadow banking sector, where they perform the function of concealing shortfalls in capital, rather than being used in new lending to the productive sector. This indicates there is significant scope to increase both corporate and effective average tax rates through international cooperation, terminate or reduce many of the subsidies, grants and tax relief to business and demand that a substantial part of cash hoardings are invested in sustainable development projects.

# Increasing labour share of national income

## Falling labour share of GDP

Austerity policies have led to a further decline in the labour share of national income, whilst a greater share of labour income is going to those with highest incomes, thus increasing inequality (Onaran and Galanis, 2012). The median labour share of national income fell from 66.1% to 61.7% between 1990 and 2009 in 26 out of 30 developed countries (Organisation for Economic Co-operation and Development, 2012).

This is a significant shift in the distribution of national income between labour (wages, salaries and fringe benefits) and capital (corporate profits, income of small businesses and professional partnerships, rents from land and property and net interest on bank deposits, bonds and loans). The trend is quantified in several studies (International Institute for Labour Studies, 2011; Onaran and Galanis, 2012; Bassanini and Manfredi, 2012; International Labour Organisation, 2013; Lansley and Reed, 2013).

Australia has the highest reduction in labour share of GDP between 1970 and 2007 (see Table 8) followed by the UK and Sweden and a narrowing of the gap in Japan and Denmark.

**Table 8: The wage share in ten advanced economies, 1970-2007**

| Country | labour share (% of GDP) | | Change |
|---|---|---|---|
| | 1970 | 2007 | |
| Australia | 60 | 53 | -7.1 |
| UK | 65 | 60 | -5.3 |
| Sweden | 66 | 61 | -4.9 |
| Canada | 59 | 55 | -3.8 |
| Germany | 59 | 55 | -3.7 |
| USA | 64 | 60 | -3.1 |
| France | 56 | 57 | +0.9 |
| Finland | 55 | 56 | +1.0 |
| Denmark | 59 | 65 | +6.1 |
| Japan | 41 | 49 | +8.2 |

*Source: Reed and Mohun Himmelweit, 2012, based on OECD data*

## Causes of falling labour share

Financialisation (the increased role of financial markets, the aggressive short-termism of financial institutions and rising indebtedness of households) was the main cause of the fall in the labour share of national income. A study of 71 countries (28 advanced and 43 developing and emerging economies) between 1970 and 2007 found financialisation accounted for a 3.3% decline in the wage share, a 1.9% decline for welfare state retrenchment, a decline of 1.3% and 0.7% for globalisation and technological change respectively in the advanced countries (Stockhammer, 2013a).

Another study had similar findings by examining data for 71 countries in two selected periods 1990-2004 and 2000-04 – financialisation contributed 46% of the fall in labour share, 25% by welfare state retrenchment and union density, 19% by globalisation and 10% for technology (International Labour Organisation, 2013). *'... the relationship between financial globalisation and the wage share is consistently negative across the majority of high-income countries'* (International Institute for Labour Studies, 2011).

The gap between productivity and pay is a key factor. *'Based on the wage data for 36 countries, we estimate that since 1999 average labour productivity has increased more than twice as much as average wages in developed economies'* – see Figure 17 (International Labour Organisation, 2013). It starkly illustrates how capital captured the bulk of the benefits of increased productivity.

**Figure 17: Trends in growth in average wages and labour productivity in developed economies (Index: 1999=100)**

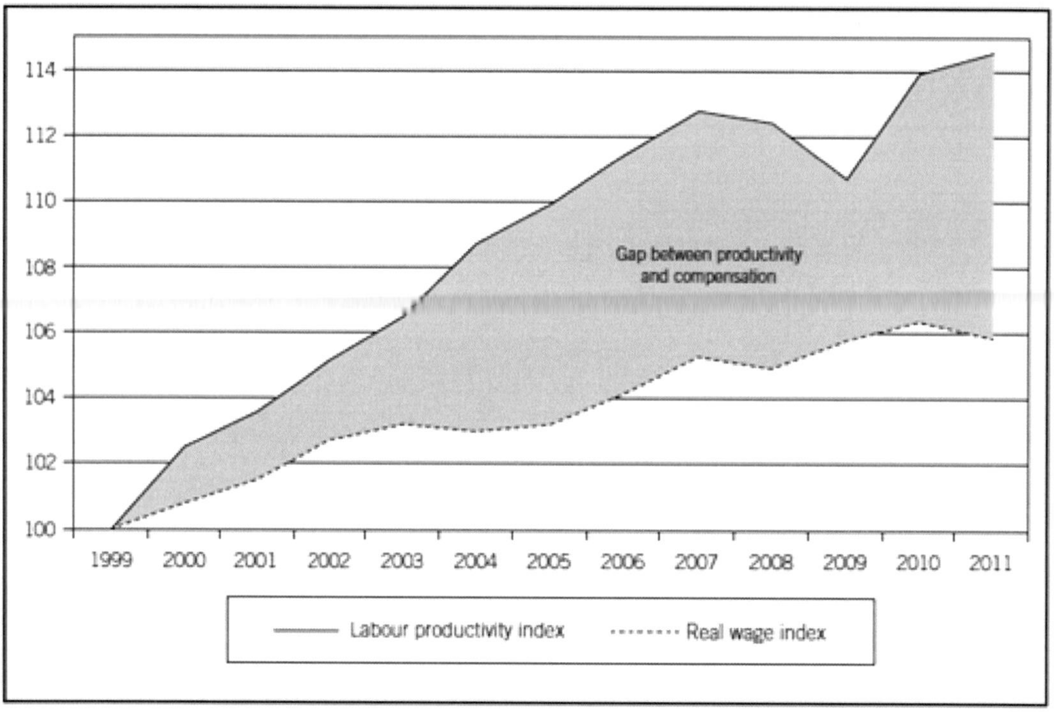

Productivity in the USA increased 245.3% between 1948 and 2010 compared to a 113% increase in hourly wage rates. Growth rates were comparable up to 1973, but after that, productivity grew strongly whilst wage rates were relatively stagnant (Mishel, 2012).

The privatisation of network industries (telecommunications, electricity, gas, airlines, railways, roads and postal services) is another contributing factor. A study of privatisation in eighteen OECD countries between 1970 and 2001 concluded *'... the wave of privatization in OECD countries is a significant part of the declining share of labour in the network industries – accounting for a fifth of the fall on average, but over half in Britain and France'* (Azmat et al, 2012). This is due to large falls in employment, offset by higher wages (outsourcing and privatisation of other services experience both job and wage cuts).

Another study concluded *'... massive privatisation of network industries since the early 1990's can explain about 33% of the decline of the labour share in these industries'* (Bassanini and Manfredi, 2012). Since many countries privatised state-owned corporations in other sectors of the economy, the impact of privatisation is probably *'... at least as important as that of globalisation'* (ibid). The reduction in bargaining power of labour contributed to the decline in the labour share of national income (International Institute for Labour Studies, 2011).

The fall in labour share of national income led to a decline in workers purchasing power, but financial deregulation provided a short-term solution for capital. Consumption booms in the US and a lesser extent in the UK, Australia and the bailout countries (Greece, Ireland, Portugal and Spain), were underpinned by soaring household debt rather than rising wages. *'... changing financial norms, new financial instruments (credit card debt, home equity lending) and deterioration of creditworthiness standards, triggered by the securitization of mortgage debt, made increasing amounts of credit available to low-income, low-wealth households, in particular.* ***Household debt thus became a substitute for higher wages as a source of demand and consumption'*** [my emphasis] (International Labour Organisation, 2013).

Not only has the labour share of national income been in decline, but inequality has been rapidly increasing within the labour share. The top 1% of US households had 59.9% of the increase in income between 1979 and 2007 compared to only 8.6% for the bottom 90.0% (Mishel and Bivens, 2011). The top 1% of incomes grew by 31.4% between 2009 and 2012 in stark contrast to only a 0.4% increase for the bottom 99% – thus the top 1% captured 95% of the income gains in this three-year period (Saez, 2013).

> *'... inequality in income distribution is one of the major causes of the crisis along with financial deregulation at a national and international scale. In the face of falling wage share across the world, a global stagnation was avoided thanks to an increase in debt, mostly private, and global imbalances. After the collapse of the debt-led model with the global recession, the wage moderation policies of the last three decades proved to be unsustainable. Reversing inequality would bring us a step closer to eliminating a major cause of the crisis; it would also be a way of making the responsible pay for the crisis'* (Onaran and Galanis, 2012).

The gap between chief executive's pay and typical worker wages is growing rapidly again after shrinking during the recession. The ratio of annual pay received by chief executives of the largest 350 U.S. firms relative to annual wages of production/nonsupervisory workers in those firms' industries was roughly 20-to-1 in 1965. By 2012, it was 273-to-1 – see Figure 18 (Economic Policy Institute, 2013b).

**Figure 18: The gap between US chief executive and typical worker wages 1965-2012**

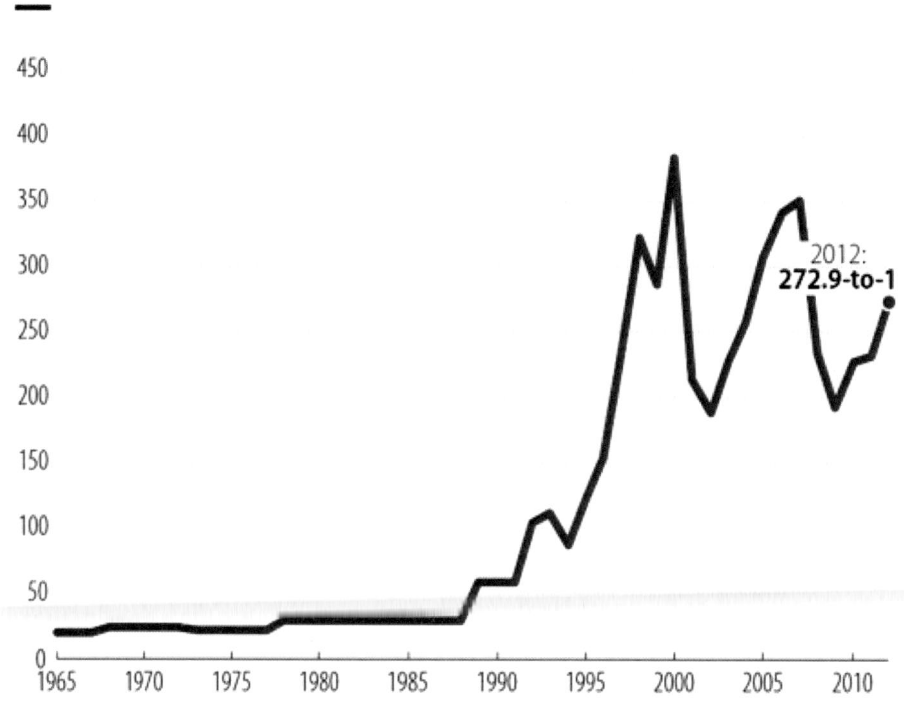


*Source: Economic Policy Institute, 2013*

## Ways to increase the labour share of national income

A quarter of US workers and one-fifth of workers in the UK, Canada, Ireland, and Germany were in low-wage jobs (earning less than two-thirds of the national median hourly wage) compared to 11.1% and 8.0% in France and Italy respectively (Schmitt, 2012). In the UK there was a significant loss of jobs in the high-productivity sector with an above-average level of output per worker, whereas 550,000 full and part-time jobs were added in the low productivity, low wage sector, mainly business services, between 2008-2011 (Martin and Rowthorn, 2012). The shift from higher to lower-wage jobs also reduced productivity.

Employers should be required to pay a living wage, and a cap imposed on excessive salaries in banks and businesses would help to increase the labour share of national income. Contract compliance, including employment conditions, minimum use of zero-hour contracts and defined benefit pensions are vitally important.

The multi-billion dollar benefits paid to working people on low incomes/wages, such as the UK Working Tax Credit and US Earned Income Tax Credit are, in effect, a public subsidy to corporate employers who will otherwise have no incentive to improve their employee's terms and conditions (See Chapter 4). These tax credits could be systematically reduced in parallel with wage increases.

Policies to create full employment, increased national minimum and living wage rates, reduction of the gender pay gap, increased trade union membership and representation, extended collective bargaining and workplace participation have an important role in increasing the labour share of national income. Pension privatisation must be strongly resisted together with all further moves to close or erode defined benefit schemes.

## Key lessons

Alternative economic stimulus strategies alone will be only partially effective. They must be accompanied by industrial investment and innovation, the reconstruction of the state and public services, more rapid reform of banks and financial markets, a radical reduction in corporate welfare and ways to increase the labour share of national income.

The fixation with rapid public debt reduction is a ploy to accelerate neoliberal transformation of the public sector and welfare state. The political focus is on public, not private debt, yet little has been done to address the continuing high level of household debt.

Trade unions, community and civil society organisations must be closely involved in the drawing up of alternative economic strategies to ensure they are comprehensive and fully incorporate their needs and interests.

Alternative economic strategies should provide a springboard for the preparation of more detailed visions, plans and strategies for sectors, services, regions and localities that could be integrated into trade union, civil and community organisation and protest movement activities.

Building coalitions and alliances and jointly developing alternative policies and integrating them into organising and action strategies should be standard practice.

More substantive and frequent interventions to challenge local policies and procurements are urgently needed in which alternative plans and policies have a key role in building public support. The financial crisis, rapidly evolving technology and demographic change mean that the status quo is rarely tenable. Alternative policies can strengthen organising and combine proactive, interventionist and defensive tactics.

Clarity of language and objectives is essential (Whitfield, 2006) in the drive to re-engage citizens in the politics of economic management. Alternative policies must be based on solidarity and public service principles rather than the fixation with individual consumption. Policies can be rapidly watered down and apparent support can vaporise at the legislative and implementation stage. It is therefore vital to retain 'ownership' of alternative policies and strategies, to constantly develop and improve them, revise their costs and benefits and assess the economic, social justice, environmental, health and employment benefits.

# Chapter 4
# Exposing causes, contradictions and conflicts

This chapter discusses the deeper causes of the financial crisis and the manufactured crises being used to further dismantle hard earned labour rights and the welfare state. The chapter examines four contradictions and conflicts evident in advancing alternative policies to austerity and neoliberalism – labour market reform, but greater dependence on the welfare state; 'smaller state' but bigger role in the economy; localism and transparency or centralisation and secrecy; and corporate welfare or public resources. It concludes by calling for a radical rethink of trade union, community and social movement organising and action strategies.

## Causes and manufactured crises

The specific causes and consequences of the 2008 crisis were set out in Chapter 1. It was a failure of financial markets and the latest in a series of economic and financial crises in the capitalist economy. Significant as they were, the ultimate causes of the 2008 financial crisis run deeper and are more profound than the failure of financial markets and deregulation.

Rising inequality is frequently cited as a key cause (Treeck and Sturn, 2012) or '*... the interaction of the effects of financial deregulation with the macroeconomic effects of rising inequality*' (Stockhammer, 2013b). A recent IMF paper concluded, '*... inequality continues to be a robust and powerful determinant both of the pace of medium-term growth and of the duration of growth spells*' and '*... there is surprisingly little evidence for the growth-destroying effects of fiscal redistribution at a macroeconomic level*' (Ostry et al, 2014).

The level of inequality is grotesque. The UK has the second highest level of inequality in the developed OECD countries, which costs the equivalent of over £39bn every year (The Equality Trust, 2014). However, the causes of persistent economic and financial crises in the capitalist economy are not only rooted in the distribution of income and wealth, but in the ownership and democratic control of the means by which income and wealth is produced. Several decades of neoliberal policies – privatisation, marketisation, deregulation and labour market 'reform' have been imposed and fervently promoted by the IMF, World Bank and OECD and were key contributory factors to the crisis and to increasing inequality.

### Manufactured crises

Austerity policies continue and there are no plans, let alone commitments, to reverse any of the public spending cuts, wage and pension cuts or other austerity measures (see Chapter 1). The scale and length of the recession is likely to lead to most negative impacts being attributed to austerity policies. This conveniently obscures more fundamental, deep-rooted problems in the capitalist economy.

President Obama's 2015 US Budget plan for non-defence discretionary spending, such as infrastructure and education, will fall from 3.1% of GDP in 2013 to just 2.2% in 2024 compared to a 3.8% average over the previous 40 years. A 42% cut in spending would have dramatic consequences and would shift investment responsibilities to already resource-strapped cities and metropolitan areas (Katz, 2014). The financial crisis of US cities is a combination of centrally imposed budget cuts; increased demand for services caused by economic recession and austerity; the property and housing market collapse, demographic change and de-industrialisation.

For example, the City of Detroit filed for bankruptcy in 2013, but the causes of the city's problems are rooted decades ago in de-industrialisation, racism and flight of the white population from the inner city to suburban townships and the structural fragmentation of US local government. Detroit is a small part (700,000 population) of a large metropolitan region of independent cities and townships (4.2m population).

A 'crisis' in US state and city pension funds has been manufactured by conservative interests in a similar way that they claim the end of the 'age of entitlement' because welfare states are 'unaffordable' and 'unsustainable'. Detroit's public pension funds were no exception, despite being well funded (92%) compared to most large cities (Long, 2013c). Police and fire service pensioners will receive 90% and other members 70% of earned pensions, but all will lose the annual cost of living increase under the city's Plan of Adjustment filed with the Bankruptcy Court in February 2014 (City of Detroit, 2014).

Corporate and right wing interests claimed US public pension funds had an annual US$46bn (£27.6bn) shortfall, but this is dwarfed by the US$120bn (£72bn) spent on corporate subsidies (Sirota, 2013). The shortfall was blamed on powerful trade unions extracting 'excessive' benefits. Some states fully funded their pension schemes, but at least 14 regularly failed to make their required annual contribution in the decade before the financial crisis (Taibbi, 2013). But the dramatic fall in share prices at the start of the financial crisis had the biggest impact with a three year US$850bn (£510bn) fall in pension assets (compared to returns equal to the interest rate on 30-year Treasury bonds) in the three years after 2007. In addition, state budget cuts reduced their pension fund contributions by a further US$80bn (£48bn). However, the record high share prices in 2013/2014 will have significantly reduced the shortfalls (Baker, 2011).

The State of Rhode Island followed the pension 'reform' path by transferring US$1bn (£0.6bn), 14% of state pension funds, for management by three Wall Street hedge funds. However, annual investment expenses increased nearly sevenfold from US$11m (£6.6m) to US$70m (£42m) and investment performance lagged 1.36%

behind the median public sector pension in the year ending 30 June 2013 (Benchmark Financial Services, 2013).

The exploitation of crises reflects the increased power of finance capital and corporate interests dictating who will pay the costs of market failure and to seek financial gain from the management of public assets. In addition, corporations exploit competition between cities to remain or relocate in order to obtain economic development tax breaks, subsidies and grants.

## Contradictions and conflicts

Advancing alternative policies (Chapter 3) will be confronted by contradictions and conflicts between the different interests of capital, such as financial institutions, outsourcing contractors and global, national and local businesses. Their respective corporate and trade organisations will vociferously oppose most, if not all, alternative policies.

## Labour market reform, but greater dependence on the welfare state

The OECD and many governments promote continued labour market reform (OECD, 2013e). This effectively means reducing the cost of labour through pay and pension cuts, and job losses. Divisions between those with relatively good quality jobs, terms and conditions and those with low pay, zero hour contracts, mini-jobs or part-time jobs with poor conditions and pensions, are the inevitable consequences of cost driven 'reforms'.

The 'Americanisation' of labour policy in Europe will have drastic economic and social consequences (Porter, 2013). It conflicts with many EU policies, such as social cohesion, reducing inequalities and improving well-being. Further reductions in the labour share of national income are likely to weaken trade union power and will increase inequalities, household debt and demands on the welfare state. The household debt/income ratio is increasing in the UK, US and Canada, but this could constrain economic demand. Mortgage, tuition fees, car purchase and credit card debt and increasing and financialising and personalising public services will shift the cost of health, social care, education on to household budgets. The lack of access to benefits would inevitably increase poverty and inequalities.

Strategies to increase labour's share of national income are essential to reduce income, health and other inequalities. Pay, pensions, working conditions and living wage standards should be advanced as a local economy and community issue and not be limited to a trade union/workplace matter.

Support for both living wage campaigns and improving terms and conditions in national agreements negotiated in collective bargaining is essential, otherwise the erosion of collective bargaining (and trade union membership) could lead to the gradual replacement of national agreements with lower but local standards. Improving minimum wages, living wages and national pay agreements are critically important to increase labour share of national income.

## 'Smaller state' but bigger role in the economy

Austerity imposed new and additional demands on the welfare state, such as increased numbers of people claiming unemployment benefits and income support, which have been exploited by neoliberals and right wing parties to challenge its affordability and sustainability. Not surprisingly, there is a common solution to the 'crises' – privatisation by hiving off social security, public pensions, welfare benefits and public infrastructure to the private sector. The same interests irreverently seek to emasculate all levels of government, ignoring the increased demands that it will generate on the state and the political and economic consequences of terminating universal provision and replacing them with residualised models.

Lower pay and pensions and the end of 'age of entitlement' will not only have drastic social and economic consequences, but will also reduce the effectiveness of the welfare state's role as an 'automatic stabiliser' to maintain aggregate demand in the economy. The next recession could be even more severe for the poor and working class families, because reduced economic demand could lead to an even deeper recession. In these circumstances the state may be forced to increase a previously reduced or capped benefits system in response to economic and/or political pressure.

The small state model conflicts with the need for a strong state to deal with market failure, address social needs, reduce inequalities, undertake industrial and infrastructure investment, tackle climate change and to regulate and manage the economy. The commodification of health, education and other core services, will impose new demands on the welfare state from those who are excluded from markets and dealing with market failure.

Neoliberal transformation is a key route to the small state. Financialising, personalising and marketising services will ultimately lead to privatisation through several pathways.

Firstly, the transfer of services to arms length companies, trusts and social enterprises means that budgets, staff and democratic control are removed from the public realm.

Secondly, outsourcing and most of the US contract cities (which outsource the bulk of services) were established long before the 2008 financial crisis. However, new models of PPP strategic partnerships (long-term, multi-service contracts) are emerging in the UK, such as whole service contracts (Whitfield, 2014). Strategic partnerships originated in ICT and corporate services, but have extended into planning, education, police, fire and rescue and property services. A slightly remodelled PPP infrastructure project model continues in the UK despite wide criticism and failures. PPPs and the infrastructure market continue to extend their global reach (Whitfield, 2010).

Reliance on new market mechanisms, such as 'value capture' in which public infrastructure projects are financed by nearby landowners who will benefit from improved infrastructure (Levenson and Istrate, 2011), are high-risk strategies. Modelled on Tax Increment Financing, these approaches rely on capturing increases in land values over 25-30 years, but are susceptible to property crashes and recession. Furthermore, increased land values could make other public and social infrastructure in the vicinity unaffordable and determine land uses/density that is not in the public interest or does not meet local needs. Impact fees, joint development, special assessments, tax increment financing, land-value taxes, transportation utility fees, and air rights are among the most widely discussed forms of value capture.

Thirdly, the growth of support for social impact bonds and a social investment market is an example of how neoliberal policies create new private markets to financialise and privatise public services for a new class of investors, backed by global capital (Whitfield, 2012a, Canadian Union for Public Employees, 2013). The idea has spread geographically and across services. The 'social investor' is a front to draw in mainstream private capital to fund social and other public services that would otherwise, at least initially, only attract outsourcing companies.

Social impact bonds create a new market for financial intermediaries, social impact bond issuers, contractors and consultants/auditors with high transaction costs syphoning off resources from service delivery; they introduce profiteering (annual returns of 7%-13%) into services for those most in need, such as troubled families and prisoners awaiting release; a payment mechanism that compares performance with existing rather than improved public services, use 'outcome' measures that are ill-defined and/or difficult to establish a cause/effect relationship; and payment by results could lead to gaming by contractors concentrating on the 'easier' users to maximise 'success'.

Fourthly, the UK voluntary sector is being drawn into competition and contracting, although a vibrant critical opposition draws on UK (National Coalition for Independent Action, 2011) and US experience (Miller 2011, Smith, 2010). The corporatisation and marketisation of the voluntary sector will lead to mergers and consolidation, the domination of commercial values, less advocacy and an increasing divide between national organisations and charities and local voluntary groups. Whilst network organisations will be able to promote policies at regional and national level, frontline organisations that have traditionally advocated on behalf of, and engaged with, those in poverty, the unemployed and working class communities, will be compromised by the dual role of contractor and support for critical opposition of the same public body.

Finally, demand management is emerging as another strategy to reduce the demand for public services and reduce costs because '*... future demand will not only outstrip current supply, but is likely to overwhelm public agencies with a set of needs that do not correspond to the service models of today, and that challenge the very basis of* *public services'* (Randle and Kippin, 2014). It claims *'... austerity creates grey areas – areas in which citizens could – or should – take more responsibility for their own behaviour: for managing, funding, or meeting their own needs or complying with initiatives designed to recognise wider community benefits'* (ibid). There are different types of demand – failure, avoidable, preventable, co-dependent and excess – the solution to the latter is claimed to range from charging to act as a deterrent or contribute to the costs, *'... punitive measures such as fines for non-compliance'* and *'... changing eligibility criteria to focus resources on the most in need'* (ibid). This is otherwise known as rationing. 'Nudge' interventions and behavioural economics are also used to reduce demand and influence choice and raise further questions.

Strategies for early intervention, transferring resources to prevention and service redesign are vitally important, but demand management has a high risk of marginalising social need whilst promoting cost reductions. It is another tool for neoliberal transformation – one of the organisations, which authored the above report, was also a prime consultant in the London Borough of Barnet's mass outsourcing programme 2010-2013! (European Services Strategy Unit, 2012).

Although PPPs, social bonds and the social investment market imply private finance, it is only upfront funding and they are entirely financed by the public sector. Pathways may require service users to pay new and higher charges, tolls and/or fees and to contribute to vouchers and personal budgets when they are insufficient to meet user needs.

The focus on the privatisation pathways detracts from the need for a new public service management to retain or rebuild the capability for in-house provision. Initiatives to innovate and improve in-house provision are becoming less frequent despite high contract failure rates, higher public sector costs, reduced quality and inequality. Changing policies and programmes have very limited effect if they are to be implemented by neoliberal public managers.

The previous UK Labour governments (under Blair and Brown) accelerated the neoliberal 'transformation' of public services, which the current Coalition have extended and embedded, for example, academies. Labour is seeking to return to power with policy programmes that are 'repeal averse', in that they only propose marginal change. For example, the previous Labour government imposed the commissioning (client/contractor split) model in the NHS, subsequently mainstreamed in the public sector by the Coalition. However, the Labour agenda is limited to improving procurement and outsourcing instead of a focus on innovation and improvement of in-house provision to pre-empt the need for procurement.

The grab for more corporate power reveals further dangers in the small state model. Nation states are being drawn into free trade agreements such as the Transatlantic Trade and Investment Partnership and the Trans Pacific Partnership. Deregulation, not trade, is the prime motive, which could lead to the dismantling of regulations implemented in the reform of banks and financial markets and impose new regulatory regimes bypassing democratic decision-making (Baker, 2014).

## Localism and transparency or centralisation and secrecy

Democratic accountability, participation, transparency and localism are widely promoted but policy-making is increasingly centralised with key roles occupied by business interests and a policy agenda dominated by marketisation and privatisation. Austerity policies imposed across Europe gave local government little 'choice' between maintaining statutory services and funding other functions and activities. Supranational bodies have imposed policies on nation states and management of the economy has been ceded to technocrats, which has eroded democratic governance.

There is wide political support to improve democratic accountability, participation and transparency; however, showpiece initiatives give the illusion of increasing local decision-making, if not control. Meanwhile, the outsourcing and privatisation policy agenda will significantly erode accountability, specifically exclude participation and will be blanketed by commercial confidentiality.

The transfer to arms length companies, social enterprises and trusts create the illusion of local accountability, but not in practice if financial decisions, policies and performance criteria are outside the control of those organisations. The fracturing and fragmenting of government and public bodies makes democratic accountability more difficult to achieve and sustain. For example, the transfer of schools from local government to nationally funded 'independent' academies and free schools operated by profit/non-profit regional or national chains replace democratically accountable local government.

Commissioning is leading to a regime of competition, commercialisation and a contract culture that erodes public service principles and values and the loss of public service staff as they are transferred to new private or voluntary sector employers. Outsourcing to profit and non-profit companies make local, city, regional and national accountability more distant than ever.

Driving down wages and pensions will further restrict participation – people will have less and less time to participate, because many would need to have multiple jobs to maintain their living standards.

## Corporate welfare or public resources

Corporate interests work ceaselessly to maintain the significant benefits they receive from corporate welfare regimes of corporate tax cuts, public subsidies and grants, tax havens and state market-making policies that increase outsourcing. They fund trade bodies, think tanks and right wing organisations to try to undermine and dismantle the welfare state and privatise public services. New models of Public Private Partnerships

(Whitfield, 2014) and the social investment market will further embed corporate welfare.

The drive for labour market 'reform' is increasing public subsidy of low pay, primarily in the private sector. The Earned Income Tax Credit (EITC) and the Working Tax Credit in the US and UK respectively are designed to provide additional financial assistance to those on low incomes. The EITC is estimated to have lifted 10.1m families out of poverty in 2012 (Harris, 2014) – claimants received an average US$2,270 (£1,360) per annum in tax credits and refunds.

Over half the taxpayers in Alabama, Georgia, and Mississippi claimed EITC. With few exceptions, almost all counties with high rates of EITC take-up are located in the South. A stream of US and foreign manufacturing plants moved to the southern states in last two decades to exploit a low wage economy and low levels of trade union membership, for example the 10.8%, 5.3% and 3.6% trade union membership respectively in the three states referred to above (Long, 2014).

More than half (52%) of the families of US frontline fast-food workers are enrolled in one or more public benefit programmes – 45% are enrolled in the EITC and received US$1.9bn (£1.2bn) in 2011. Front-line fast-food workers received a further US$5bn (£3bn) in food stamp benefits, Medicaid and Children's Health Insurance Program benefits of US$7,650 (£4,590) per family per annum, as a result of employers low wage practices (Allegretto et al, 2013). This is a blatant example of corporate welfare where private companies rely on the state and other taxpayers to finance/bolster their corporate profits.

The UK's Working Tax Credit is a means-tested benefit for working families. In-work poverty accounted for the majority of people in poverty in the UK in 2011/12 (MacInnes et al, 2013). In-work poverty began to rise around 2003/04 increasing to 6.7m people in poverty with three quarters ([illegible]m) working age adults in work in 2011/12. There were 4.6m low paid jobs in the UK in 2012 (ibid). Low pay alone is not the only determinant of poverty as the cost of housing, spouse income and family size determine household income and expenditure.

These programmes clearly lift many families out of poverty, but they equally subsidise private and public sector employers low wage policies. It is not possible to identify the specific proportion of these programmes related to low wages, but with annual costs of US$59bn and £21bn in the US and UK respectively, the corporate subsidies are substantial. The drive for further labour market 'reform' and cost reduction will inevitably increase public subsidy of employer's low wage strategies.

## Rethinking strategies

A radical rethink of trade union, community and civil society objectives, values and action strategies is urgently required, drawing on the lessons learnt in Chapter 2. It should strengthen organising, build alliances that engage members and organisations in thinking about their future, their quality of life, the action is needed to achieve their aspirations and how inequalities can be radically reduced. Austerity and the drive for 'labour market reform' has highlighted that trade union membership alone is limited in reducing the risk of job loss and cuts in terms and conditions. Therefore, trade unions and members must adopt new strategies that build wider support locally and nationally.

Organising to build social movements may start with allegiance to websites, blogs and twitter, but must engage people in collective action and ultimately retain their allegiance to a 'movement', if not to some form of organisation. Action against austerity highlighted the limitations of trade unionism acting in isolation, which makes building alliances with community and civil society organisations even more imperative (see Chapter 3).

Alternative policies must not be limited to restoring what was lost through cuts and closures or replacing what was rundown, but the policies and visions that are needed to achieve fundamental political, economic, social and environmental change. The language and ideology of austerity and neoliberalism must be replaced with transformative demands and policies to radically reconstruct the welfare state and public services.

Re-municipalisation and the return of assets to public ownership will have limited effect if the opportunity is not taken to radically change public management and redefine what public ownership means in practice. Reconstruction of public services and the welfare state must be centred on democratic accountability, participation and transparency; service innovation, improvement and investment; a new public service management; implementation of public service principles and values and regular review and scrutiny.

The 10-point strategy set out in Chapter 3 is a starting point and needs to be supported by a more substantive longer-term interventionist strategy combined with resources to provide organising and technical support for action strategies. The longer-term strategy should prioritise organising in the workplace, community and social movements with the objective of forging more powerful local, national and international coalitions and alliances. User/community and staff/trade union involvement in the planning, design and service delivery is vitally important.

There is an urgent need to build capacity for critical analysis and the ability to prepare alternative visions, plans and policies in order to intensify intervention in policy-making and build political support. Alternative policies and strategies must be developed at all levels from service innovation and improvement plans to retain local in-house provision to national and international economic, social and environmental policies. They should articulate a vision of industrial investment and democracy, together with innovation and investment in public goods and provision.

# References


Aglietta, M. (2012) The European Vortex, *New Left Review*, 75, May-June, 15-36.

Allegretto, S., Doussard, M., Graham-Squire, D., Jacobs, K., Thompson, D. and Thompson, J. (2013) *Fast Food, Poverty Wages: The Public Cost of Low-Wage Jobs in the Fast-Food Industry,* Center for Labour Research and Education, University of California Berkeley, http://laborcenter.berkeley.edu/publiccosts/fast_food_poverty_wages.pdf

Allen, K. and O'Boyle, B. (2013) *Austerity Ireland: The Failure of Irish Capitalism,* Pluto Press, London.

Almalki, M., FitzGerald, G. and Clark M. (2012) *The relationship between quality of work life and turnover intention of primary health care nurses in Saudi Arabia,* BMC Health Services Research, 12: 314.

Alternative Trade Mandate (2013) *Trade: time for a new vision: The Alternative Trade Mandate,* September, http://www.alternativetrademandate.org/wp-content/uploads/2013/09/ATM-Document-Final-EN.pdf

Alvarez, P, Manetto, F. and Hernandez, J.A. (2013) *Anatomy of an 'escrache', El Pais,* 13 April, http://elpais.com/elpais/2013/04/14/inenglish/1365953446_509059.html

American Federation of Labor and Congress of Industrial Organisations (2013) *Building on AFL-CIO Commitment to Broaden Labor Movement,* Press Release, 25 September, Washington DC, http://www.aflcio.org/Press-Room/Press-Releases/AFL-CIO-USAS-Establish-National-Partnership

Andronikidou, A. and Kovras, I. (2012) Cultures of Rioting and Anti-Systemic Politics in Southern Europe, *West European Politics,* 35:4, 707-725.

Angelos, J. and Adam, N. (2013) 'Minijobs' Lift Employment But Mask German Weakness, *Wall Street Journal,* 29 May,
http://online.wsj.com/news/articles/SB10001424127887324682204578512782697519080

Aronowitz, S. (2011) One, Two Many Madisons: The war on public sector workers, *New Labor Forum,* 20(2), 15-21

Atkinson, T., Lutrell, D. and Rosenblum, H. (2013) *How Bad Was It? The Costs and Consequences of the 2007–09 Financial Crisis,* Staff Paper No. 20, July, Federal Reserve Bank of Dallas, http://dallasfed.org/assets/documents/research/staff/staff1301.pdf

Auerbach, A. and Gorodnichenko, Y. (2011) *Fiscal Multipliers in Recession and Expansion,* National Bureau of Economic Research Working Paper 17447, Cambridge, MA,
http://www.nber.org/papers/w17447

Australian Government Treasury (2013) Risks to the Sustainability of Australia's Corporate Tax Base, Scoping Paper, July, http://www.treasury.gov.au/PublicationsAndMedia/Publications/2013/Aus-Corporate-Tax-Base-Sustainability

Azmat, G., Manning, A. and Van Reenen, J. (2012) Privatization and the Decline of Labour's Share: International Evidence from Network Industries, *Economica,* 79, 470-492.

Badiou, Alain (2013) The Greek Symptom: Debt, Crisis and the Crisis of the Left, *Radical Philosophy* 181 http://www.radicalphilosophy.com/article/our-contemporary-impotence

Baker, D. (2011) *The Origins and Severity of the Public Pension Crisis,* Center for Economic and Policy Research, Washington DC, http://www.cepr.net/documents/publications/pensions-2011-02.pdf

Baker, D. (2014) TTIP: It's Not About Trade! *Social Europe Journal,* 13 February, http://www.social-europe.eu/2014/02/ttip/

Ball, L., Furceri, D., Leigh, D. and Loungani, P. (2013) *The distributional effects of fiscal austerity,* Working Paper No. 129, June, United Nations Department of Economic and Social Affairs, New York, http://www.un.org/esa/desa/papers/2013/wp129_2013.pdf

Barker, A. and Spiegel, P. (2013) Europe agrees to pool control of bank wind-ups, *Financial Times,* 18 December, http://www.ft.com/intl/cms/s/0/ed8cc406-681d-11e3-8ada-00144feabdc0.html?siteedition=intl#axzz2o7ZDZmCC

Basel Committee on Banking Supervision (2010) *An assessment of the long-term economic impact of stronger capital and liquidity requirements,* Bank for International Settlements, Basel, http://www.bis.org/publ/bcbs173.pdf

Bassanini, A. and Manfredi T. (2012) *Capital's Grabbing Hand? A Cross-Country/Cross-Industry Analysis of the Decline of the Labour Share,* OECD Social, Employment and Migration Working Papers, No. 133, OECD Publishing. http://dx.doi.org/10.1787/5k95zqsf4bxt-en

Batini, N., Callegari, G. and Melina, G. (2012) *Successful Austerity in the United States, Europe and Japan,* IMF Working Paper WP/12/190, Washington DC, http://www.imf.org/external/pubs/ft/wp/2012/wp12190.pdf

Beatty, C. and Fothergill, S. (2013) *Hitting the poorest places hardest: The local and regional impact of welfare reform,* Centre for Regional Economic and Social Research, Sheffield Hallam University, http://www.shu.ac.uk/research/cresr/sites/shu.ac.uk/files/hitting-poorest-places-hardest_0.pdf

Benchmark Financial Services Inc (2013) *Rhode Island Public Pension Reform: Wall Street's License to Steal,* October, for Rhode Island Council 94, American Federation of State, County and Municipal Employees http://www.ricouncil94.org/Portals/0/Uploads/Documents/Rhode%20Island%20X.pdf

Benski, T., Langman, L., Perugorria, I. and Tejerina, B. (2013) From the street and squares to social movements studies: What have we learned? *Current Sociology,* 61(4), 541-561.

Berry, J. and Worthen, H. (2012) Faculty Organising in the Higher Education Industry: Tackling the for-profit business model, *Working USA: The Journal of Labor and Society,* vol. 15, September, 427-440.

Bivens, J. (2012) *Public Investment: The next 'new thing' for powering economic growth,* Briefing Paper No. 338, Economic Policy Institute, April, Washington DC, http://s4.epi.org/files/2012/bp338-public-investments.pdf

Blanchard, O. and Leigh, D. (2013) *Growth Forecast Errors and Fiscal Multipliers,* IMF Working Paper WP/13/1, January, Washington DC, http://www.imf.org/external/pubs/ft/wp/2013/wp1301.pdf

Blyth, M. (2013a) *Austerity: The History of a Dangerous Idea,* Oxford University Press, New York.

Blyth, M. (2013b) The austerity delusion: why a bad idea won over the west, *Foreign Affairs,* 92.3, May-June.

Borsos, J. (2012) Wisconsin: Protest, Insurgency, Electoral Politics and Labor's Future, *Working USA: The Journal of Labor and Society,* vol. 15, September, 441-446.

Boyer, R. (2012) The four fallacies of contemporary austerity policies: the lost Keynesian legacy, *Cambridge Journal of Economics,* 36, 283-312.

Bristol & District Anti-Cuts Alliance (2013) *The Future of Bristol & District Anti-Cuts Alliance,* 2 July, http://www.indymedia.org.uk/en/2013/07/511082.html

Brown, S. and Lam, S. (2008) A Meta-Analysis of Relationships Linking Employee Satisfaction to Customer Responses, *Journal of Retailing,* 84 (3), 243-255.

Brunsden, J. (2013) *Banks' Off-Balance-Sheet Risks Come Under Basel Scrutiny,* Bloomberg, 30 September, http://www.bloomberg.com/news/2013-09-29/banks-face-basel-debt-limit-capturing-off-balance-sheet-risks.html

Buck, T. (2013) EU court strikes down Spain's eviction law, *Financial Times,* 15 March, http://www.ft.com/intl/cms/s/0/16e37aca-8ca5-11e2-8ee0-00144feabdc0.html#axzz2jHmB5qEd

Burke, M. (2013) The cash hoard of Western companies, *Socialist Economic Bulletin,* 21 October, http://socialisteconomicbulletin.blogspot.co.uk/2013/10/the-cash-hoard-of-western-companies.html

Calcagno, A. (2012) Can Austerity Work? *Review of Keynesian Economics,* Inaugural Issue, Autumn, pp24-36.

Callinicos, A. (2012) Contradictions of Austerity, *Cambridge Journal of Economics,* 36, 65-77.

Camfield, D. (2012) Quebec's 'Red Square' Movement: The story so far, *New Socialist,* 5 August, http://newsocialist.org/635-quebec-sredsquaremovement

Campaign Against Climate Change (2010) *One Million Climate Jobs: Solving the economic and environmental crises,* London, http://www.climate-change-jobs.org/node/14

Canada Revenue Agency (2012) *Statistics Canada Study on the Underground Economy in Canada,* 1992-2009, http://www.cra-arc.gc.ca/nwsrm/fctshts/2012/m09/fs120927-eng.html

Canadian Center for Policy Alternatives (2013) *Alternative Federal Budget* 2013, Ottawa, https://www.policyalternatives.ca/afb2013

Canadian Union for Public Employees (2013) Submission to Human Resources and Skills Development Canada, January, Ottawa,
http://cupe.ca/social-impact-bonds-wrong-model-address-homelessness-unemployment-and-poverty

Cantin, E. (2012) The Politics of Austerity and the Conservative Offensive against US Public Sector Unions, 2008-2012, *Industrial Relations,* 67-4, 612-632.

Celuba, R. and Feige, E.L. (2011) *America's Underground Economy: Measuring the size, growth and determinants of Income tax evasion in the US,* http://www.ssc.wisc.edu/econ/archive/wp2011-1.pdf

Center for Public Integrity (2012) *The 'Citizens United' decision and why it matters,* 18 October, Washington DC, http://www.publicintegrity.org/2012/10/18/11527/citizens-united-decision-and-why-it-matters

Central Bank of Ireland (2013) *Residential Mortgage Arrears and Repossessions Statistics: Q1 2013,* 21 June, Dublin, http://www.centralbank.ie/press-area/press-releases/pages/mortgagearrearsand repossessionsstatisticsq12013.aspx

Centre for Retail Research (2013) *Who's gone bust in retailing* 2010-2013? http://www.retailresearch.org/whosegonebust.php

Cerrillo Vidal, J.A. (2013) From general strike to social strike: movement alliances and innovative actions in the November 2012 Spanish general strike, *Interface,* Vol. 5(2), November, 39-46.

Chicago Teachers Union (2013) *Hundreds rally and march against CPS budget cuts, revenue shortcomings,* Press Release 26 June,
http://www.ctunet.com/blog/hundreds-rally-and-march-against-cps-budget-cuts-revenue-shortcomings

CIDOB (2013) *Profile: the Mortgage-Affected Citizens Platform, a Grassroots Organization at the Forefront of the Social Protests,* June, Barcelona,
http://www.cidob.org/publications/articulos/spain_in_focus/june_2013/profile_the_mortgage_affected _citizens_platform_a_grassroots_organization_at_the_forefront_of_the_social_protests

City of Detroit (2014) *Overview of Detroit's Plan of Adjustment,* 21 February,
http://www.detroitmi.gov/Portals/0/docs/EM/Announcements/Summary_PlanOfAdjustment.pdf

Cole, A. and Gasper, P. (2012) Wisconsin: From the uprising to Recall Walker, *International Socialist Review,* No. 83, May, http://isreview.org/issue/83/wisconsin-uprising-recall-walker

Collins, J. (2012) Theorizing Wisconsin's 2011 protests: Community-based unionism confronts accumulation by dispossession, *American Ethnologist,* Vol. 39, No.1, 6-20.

Compass (2011) Plan B: *A good economy for a good society,* edited by Howard Reed and Neal Lawson, October, London,
http://www.compassonline.org.uk/wp-content/uploads/2013/05/Compass_Plan_B_web1.pdf

Compass (2013) *Invest to Grow: a spending review to get Britain moving,* June, London,
http://www.compassonline.org.uk/wp-content/uploads/2013/06/C1_Compass_InvestPaperv4.pdf

Confederation of German Trade Unions (2012) *A Marshall Plan for Europe: Proposal by the DGB for an economic stimulus, investment and development programme for Europe,* December, Berlin, http://www.fesdc.org/pdf/A-Marshall-Plan-for-Europe_EN.pdf

Congressional Budget Office (2012) *Estimated Impact of the American Recovery and Reinvestment Act on Employment and Economic Output from October 2011 Through December 2011,* February, Washington DC, http://www.cbo.gov/sites/default/files/cbofiles/attachments/02-22-ARRA.pdf

Corporate Europe Observatory (2013) *A transatlantic corporate bill of rights – investor privileges in EU-US trade deal threaten public interest,* October, Brussels,
http://corporateeurope.org/sites/default/files/attachments/transatlantic-corporate-bill-of-rights-oct13.pdf

Council of Mortgage Lenders (2012) *Equity position of borrowers has improved,* 30 October, London, http://www.cml.org.uk/cml/publications/newsandviews/125/470

Creditreform Economic Research Unit (2012) *Insolvencies in Europe 2011-2012,* http://www.creditreform.com/fileadmin/user_upload/CR-International/local_documents/Analysen/Insolvencies_in_Europe_2011-12.pdf

Danson, M., McAlpine, R., Spicker, P. and Sullivan, W. (2012) *The Case for Universalism: An assessment of the evidence on the effectiveness and efficiency of the universal welfare state,* Jimmy Reid Foundation,
http://reidfoundation.org/wp-content/uploads/2012/12/The-Case-for-Universalism.pdf

Davy Research (2013) *Ireland's deteriorating mortgage arrears crisis,* 30 July, Dublin, http://www.davy.ie/research-and-insights/article?id=Davy_Morning_Equity_Briefing_01082014_moneBLinkMrkComm.htm

Davy Select (2014) *Market Comment Irish households continue to pay down debt at a rapid pace,* 31 January, http://www.davyselect.ie/news/article_7386.html

Davey, M. and Zeleny, J. (2012) Walker Survives Wisconsin Recall Vote, *New York Times,* 5 June, http://www.nytimes.com/2012/06/06/us/politics/walker-survives-wisconsin-recall-effort.html

Dean, A. (2012) Mobilizing the Unorganized: Is 'Working America' the way forward? *New Labor Forum,* 21(1) Winter, 61-69.

Deloitte (2013) *CFTC and EU OTC Derivatives Regulation: An Outcomes-based Comparison,* London,
http://www.deloitte.com/assets/Dcom-UnitedKingdom/Local%20Assets/Documents/Industries/Financial%20Services/uk-fs-cftc-eu.pdf

Democracy Now! (2012) *Maple Spring: Nearly 1,000 Arrested as Mass Quebec Student Strike Passes 100th Day,* 25 May, http://www.democracynow.org/2012/5/25/maple_spring_nearly_1_000_arrested

Demos (2013) *Disabled people set to lose £28.3bn of support,*
http://www.demos.co.uk/press_releases/destinationunknownapril2013

Der Spiegel (2012) *Window Dressing for Hollande: The Empty Promise of Europe's 'Growth Pact',* 27 June, http://www.spiegel.de/international/europe/the-eu-s-new-growth-pact-a-841243.html

Deutsche Bank (2013) Privatisation in the euro area: Differing attitudes towards public assets, *Research Briefing,* 20 August, Frankfurt, http://www.dbresearch.com/PROD/DBR_INTERNET_EN-PROD/PROD0000000000318583/Privatisation+in+the+euro+area%3A++Differing+attitudes+towards+public+assets.pdf

DiNovella, E. (2012) What Conservatives Learned from Labor Fights in Wisconsin and Ohio, *The Progressive,* 11 February,
http://progressive.org/what_conservatives_learned-from_labor_fights_in_wisconsin_and_ohio.html

Duffy, S. (2014) *Counting the Cuts, Campaign for a Fair Society,*
http://www.centreforwelfarereform.org/library/type/pdfs/counting-the-cuts.html

Early, S. (2013) AFL-CIO Convention: Leaving Existing Members Behind? *Socialist Project, E-Bulletin No 880,* 18 September, http://www.socialistproject.ca/bullet/880.php

Economic Policy Institute (2013a) *Four Years into Recovery, Austerity's Toll is At Least 3 Million Jobs,* Josh Bivens and Heidi Shierholz, 3 July, Washington DC, http://www.epi.org/blog/years-recovery-austeritys-toll-3-million/

Economic Policy Institute (2013b) *The Thirteen most important charts of 2013,* Washington DC, http://www.epi.org/publication/top-charts-2013/

Elola, J. (2012) Where did the 15-M movement go? *El Pais,* 9 May, http://elpais.com/elpais/2012/05/09/inenglish/1336575923_876352.html

Equal Times (2013) *'No' to the privatisation of Madrid's hospitals,* 27 September, http://www.equaltimes.org/no-to-the-privatisation-of-madrid#.VCaD5b73VSw

Erne, R. (2013) Let's accept a smaller slice of a shrinking cake. The Irish Congress of Trade Unions and Irish public sector unions in crisis, *Transfer: European Review of Labour and Research,* 19(3) 425-430.

EuroMemo Group (2012) *European integration at the crossroads: Democratic deepening for stability, solidarity and social justice,* EuroMemorandum 2012, http://www2.euromemorandum.eu/uploads/euromemorandum_2012.pdf

EuroMemo Group (2013) *The deepening crisis in the European Union: The need for a fundamental change,* EuroMemorandum 2013, http://www2.euromemorandum.eu/uploads/euromemorandum_2013.pdf

EuroMemo Group (2014) *The deepening divisions in Europe and the need for a radical alternative to EU policies,* EuroMemorandum 2014, http://www.euromemo.eu/euromemorandum/euromemorandum_2014/index.html

European Commission (2013a) *European Economic Forecast: Winter 2013,* Brussels, http://ec.europa.eu/economy_finance/publications/european_economy/2013/pdf/ee1_en.pdf

European Commission (2013b) *Commission's roadmap for tackling the risks inherent in shadow banking,* Press Release, 4 September, Brussels, http://europa.eu/rapid/press-release_IP-13-812_en.htm?locale=en

European Commission (2013c) *Taxation of the financial sector,* Brussels, http://ec.europa.eu/taxation_customs/taxation/other_taxes/financial_sector/

European Commission (2013d) *Study to quantify and analyse the VAT Gap in the EU-27 Member States,* http://ec.europa.eu/taxation_customs/resources/documents/common/publications/studies/vat-gap.pdf

European Council (2012) *European Council 28/29 June: Conclusions,* EUCO 76/12, 29 June, Brussels, http://www.consilium.europa.eu/uedocs/cms_data/docs/pressdata/en/ec/131388.pdf

European Public Services Union (2010) *The wrong target – how governments are making public sector workers pay for the crisis,* Brussels, http://www.epsu.org/IMG/pdf/Pay_cuts_report.pdf

European Securities and Markets Authority (2013) *Final Report: ESMA's technical advice on the evaluation of the Regulation (EU) 236/2012 of the European Parliament and of the Council on short selling and certain aspects of credit default swaps,* 3 June, Paris, http://www.esma.europa.eu/system/files/2013-614_final_report_on_ssr_evaluation.pdf

European Services Strategy Unit (2012) *Costs and consequences of a One Barnet Commissioning Council,* June, http://www.european-services-strategy.org.uk//news/2012/commissioning-council-plan-exposed/costs-and-consequences-of-commissioning-council.pdf

European Trade Union Confederation (2013) *A New Plan for Europe: ETUC Plan for investment, sustainable growth and quality jobs,* 7 November, Brussels, http://www.etuc.org/IMG/pdf/EN-A-new-path-for-europe.pdf

Eurostat (2013a) *Euro area government debt up to 92.2% of GDP,* July,
http://epp.eurostat.ec.europa.eu/cache/ITY_PUBLIC/2-22072013-AP/EN/2-22072013-AP-EN.PDF

Eurostat (2013b) *Business investment rate down to 19.7% in the euro area and to 19.6% in the EU27,* 29 April,
http://epp.eurostat.ec.europa.eu/cache/ITY_PUBLIC/2-29042013-BP/EN/2-29042013-BP-EN.PDF

Eurostat (2013c) *Euro area unemployment rate at 12.2%,* News Release, 2 July,
http://epp.eurostat.ec.europa.eu/cache/ITY_PUBLIC/3-01072013-BP/EN/3-01072013-BP-EN.PDF

Eurostat (2013d) *Taxation Trends in the European Union,* 2013 Edition,
http://epp.eurostat.ec.europa.eu/cache/ITY_OFFPUB/KS-DU-13-001/EN/KS-DU-13-001-EN.PDF

Fabricant, M. (2011) Reimagining Labor: The Lessons of Wisconsin, *Working USA: The Journal of Labor and Society,* Vol. 14, June, 235-241.

Farnsworth, K. (2014) *Corporate Welfare under the Spotlight: British Public Policies for Private Businesses,* Oxford, Oxfam.

Financial Times (2011) *Financial pain in Europe,* 17 October,
http://www.ft.com/intl/cms/s/0/feb598a8-f8e8-11e0-a5f7-00144feab49a.html#axzz2aL1ZocaS

Financial Times (2012a) *Icelandic bank pair jailed for five years,* 12 December,
http://www.ft.com/intl/cms/s/0/eab58f7e-6345-11e3-a87d-00144feabdc0.html#axzz2pK2vO7at

Financial Times (2012b) *France launches public investment bank,* 17 October,
http://www.ft.com/intl/[illegible]-1866-11e2-80e9-00144feabdc0.html?siteedition=intl#axzz2o7ZDZmCC

Financial Times (2013a) *Funding for Infrastructure projects dwindles,* 10 February,
http://www.ft.com/intl/cms/s/0/66eea816-7128-11e2-9b5c-00144feab49a.html#axzz2bpbVhfGo

Financial Times (2013b) *EU sets out framework for banking union,* 11 December,
http://www.ft.com/intl/cms/s/0/f65fa1ee-61e6-11e3-aa02-00144feabdc0.html?siteedition=intl#axzz2n9Dxvkox

Financial Stability Board (2013a) *Global Shadow Banking Monitoring Report 2013,* 14 November, Basel, http://www.financialstabilityboard.org/publications/r_131114.pdf

Financial Stability Board (2013b) *Credit Rating Agencies Reducing reliance and strengthening oversight* Progress report to the St Petersburg G20 Summit, 29 August,
http://www.financialstabilityboard.org/publications/r_130829d.pdf

Fine, J. (2011) Worker Centers: Entering a new stage of growth and development, *New Labor Forum,* 20(3) 45-53.

Fitch Ratings (2013) *Fitch: Iceland Debt Relief Programme Appears Fiscally Neutral,* 6 December, London, https://www.fitchratings.com/creditdesk/press_releases/detail.cfm?pr_id=810945

G20 (2010) The *G20 Toronto Summit Declaration,* June 26-27, http://www.treasury.gov/resource-center/international/Documents/The%20G-20%20Toronto%20Summit%20Declaration.pdf

G20 (2013) *G20 Leaders' Declaration,* 6 September, St Petersburg, Russia, http://www.g20.utoronto.ca/2013/2013-0906-declaration.html

Geelan, T. (2013) Responses of trade union confederations to the youth employment crisis, *Transfer: European Review of Labour and Research,* 19(3) 399-413.

Governing the States and Localities (2013) *Bankrupt Cities,* Municipalities List and Map, 18 July, http://www.governing.com/gov-data/municipal-cities-counties-bankruptcies-and-defaults.html

Government Accountability Office (2008) *Tax Administration: Comparison of the Reported Tax Liabilities of Foreign- and U.S.-Controlled Corporations,* 1998-2005, GAO-08-957, July, Washington DC, http://www.gao.gov/assets/280/278562.pdf

Government Accountability Office (2013a) *Financial Crisis Losses and Potential Impacts of the Dodd-Frank Act, GAO-13-180,* January, Washington DC, http://www.gao.gov/assets/660/651322.pdf

Government Accountability Office (2013b) *Corporate Income Tax: Effective Tax Rates Can Differ Significantly from the Statutory Rate,* GAO-13-520, May, Washington DC, http://www.gao.gov/assets/660/654957.pdf

Government of Spain (2013) *Spain's Structural Reform and Economic Policy Programme,* Ministerio De Economia Y Competitividad, Madrid, http://www.tesoro.es/doc/Presentacion/130601%20Kingdom%20of%20Spain%20(REV).pdf

Griffiths-Jones, S. and Kollatz-Ahen, M. (2013) From Austerity to Growth – One lost Year and the Danger to Lose More, 31 July, *Social Europe,* http://www.social-europe.eu/2013/07/from-austerity-to-growth-one-lost-year-and-the-danger-to-lose-more/

Hall, D. (2012) *Re-municipalising municipal services in Europe, Update,* November, Public Services International Research Unit, http://www.psiru.org/publications

Hall, D. (2013) *Austerity, economic growth, multipliers – and a radical solution to the banking and fiscal crisis,* Public Services International Research Unit, March, London, http://www.psiru.org/reports/austerity-economic-growth-multipliers-—and-radical-solution-banking-and-fiscal-crises

Harris, B. (2014) *Variation in EITC Take-up,* County by County, Brookings Institution, 30 January, Washington DC, http://www.brookings.edu/blogs/up-front/posts/2014/01/30-variation-eitc-takeup-county-harris

Harvey, D. (2010) *The Enigma of Capital and the Crises of Capitalism,* Profile Books, London.

Hastings, A., Bailey, N., Besemer, K., Bramely, G., Gannon, M. and Watkins, D. (2013) *Coping with the cuts? Local government and poorer communities,* Joseph Rowntree Foundation, York, http://www.jrf.org.uk/sites/files/jrf/local-government-communities-full.pdf

Hau, H. (2011) *Europe's €200 billion reverse wealth tax explained,* University of Geneva, VOX, 27 July, http://www.voxeu.org/article/eurozone-bailout-taxpayer-transfer-wealthy

Hennessy, T. and Stanford, J. (2013) *More Harm Than Good: Austerity's Impact in Ontario,* Canadian Center for Policy Alternatives, http://www.policyalternatives.ca/sites/default/files/uploads/publications/Ontario%20Office/2013/03/More%20Harm%20Than%20Good_0.pdf

Henwood, D. (2012a) *Walker's victory, un-sugar-coated,* 6 June, LBO News from Doug Henwood http://lbo-news.com/2012/06/06/walkers-victory-un-sugar-coated/

Henwood, D. (2012b) *Sam Gindin on the crisis in labor,* Interview, 18 June, http://lbo-news.com/2012/06/18/sam-gindin-on-the-crisis-in-labor/

Herndon, T., Ash, M. and Pollin, R. (2013) *Does High Public Debt Consistently Stifle Economic Growth? A Critique of Reinhart and Rogoff,* Political Economy Research Institute, University of Massachusetts Amherst, April, http://www.peri.umass.edu/fileadmin/pdf/working_papers/working_papers_301-350/WP322.pdf

Hetherington, P. (2013) Councils generate own power to take on the big six energy firms, 4 December, *The Guardian,* http://www.theguardian.com/society/2013/dec/04/councils-generate-own-power-big-six-energy-fuel-poverty

Hills, J., Cunliffe, J., Gambaro, L. and Obolenskaya, P. (2013) *Winners and Losers in the Crisis: The Changing Anatomy of Economic Inequality in the UK 2007-2010,* Social Policy in Cold Climate, Research Report 2, June, London, http://sticerd.lse.ac.uk/dps/case/spcc/rr02.pdf

HM Revenue & Customs (2013) *Measuring Tax Gaps,* 2013 edition, October, London, http://www.hmrc.gov.uk/statistics/tax-gaps/mtg-2013.pdf

HM Treasury (2014) *Budget 2014,* HC 1104, 19 March, London, https://www.gov.uk/government/uploads/system/uploads/attachment_data/file/293759/37630_Budget_2014_Web_Accessible.pdf

Holland, D. and Portes, J. (2012) Self-defeating Austerity? *National Institute Economic Review,* October, vol. 222: No. 1, F4.

Hope, M. (2012) United Against the Austerity Agenda, *Briarpatch,* May-June, 21-25.

Hungerford, T. and Thiess, R. (2013) *The Earned Income Tax Credit and the Child Tax Credit,* 25 September, Economic Policy Institute, Washington DC, http://www.epi.org/publication/ib370-earned-income-tax-credit-and-the-child-tax-credit-history-purpose-goals-and-effectiveness/

Hurley, M. and Gindin, S. (2011) The assault on public services: will unions lament the attacks or fight back? Chapter in Yates, M.D., *Wisconsin Uprising: Labor Fights Back,* Monthly Review Press, New York.

Hurley, M. and Gindin, S. (2011) T*he Assault on Public Services: Will Unions Lament the Attacks or Lead a Fightback?* E-Bulletin No. 516, 14 June, http://www.socialistproject.ca/bullet/516.php

Inman, P. (2014) Spending cap won't tackle causes of welfare dependency, say critics, *The Guardian,* 19 March, http://www.theguardian.com/uk-news/2014/mar/19/welfare-spending-cap-hit-disabled-low-paid

Institute for Fiscal Studies (2013) *Autumn Statement 2013,* Presentation by Carl Emmerson, http://www.ifs.org.uk/budgets/as2013/as2013_carl.pdf

Institute for Fiscal Studies (2014) *The IFS Green Budget,* February, London, http://www.ifs.org.uk/budgets/gb2014/gb2014.pdf

International Institute for Labour Studies (2011) *World of Work Report 2011:* Making Markets Work for Jobs, Geneva, http://www.ilo.org/wcmsp5/groups/public/@dgreports/@dcomm/@publ/documents/publication/wcms_166021.pdf

International Labour Organisation (2013) *Global Wage Report 2012/13: Wages and equitable growth,* Geneva, http://www.ilo.org/wcmsp5/groups/public/---dgreports/---dcomm/---publ/documents/publication/wcms_194843.pdf

International Monetary Fund (2009) *The State of Public Finances: Outlook and Medium-Term Policies After the 2008 Crisis,* March, Washington DC, http://www.imf.org/external/np/pp/eng/2009/030609.pdf

International Monetary Fund (2012a) *World Economic Outlook 2012,* October, Washington DC, http://www.imf.org/external/pubs/ft/weo/2012/02/pdf/text.pdf

International Monetary Fund (2012b) *World Economic Outlook: Growth resuming, Dangers Remain,* April, Washington DC, http://www.imf.org/external/pubs/ft/weo/2012/01/pdf/text.pdf

International Monetary Fund (2013a) *United Kingdom – 2013 Article IV Consultation Concluding Statement of the Mission,* 22 May, http://www.imf.org/external/np/ms/2013/052213.htm

International Monetary Fund (2013b) *IMF Executive Board Concludes 2013 Article IV Consultation with Spain,* 2 August, Washington DC, http://www.imf.org/external/np/sec/pr/2013/pr13292.htm

International Monetary Fund (2013c) *Fiscal Monitor: Taxing Times, October,* Washington DC, http://www.imf.org/external/pubs/ft/fm/2013/02/pdf/fm1302.pdf

International Monetary Fund (2013d) *Fiscal Monitor: Fiscal Adjustment in an Uncertain World,* April, Washington DC, http://www.imf.org/external/pubs/ft/fm/2013/01/pdf/fm1301.pdf

International Monetary Fund (2013e) *Iceland – Concluding Statement of an IMF mission for the 2013 Article IV Consultation and the Third Post-Program Monitoring Discussion,* 14 June, Washington DC, http://www.imf.org/external/np/ms/2013/061413a.htm

International Monetary Fund (2013f) *Iceland: 2013 Article IV Consultation and Third Post-Program Monitoring Discussions,* August, Washington DC, http://www.imf.org/external/pubs/ft/scr/2013/cr13256.pdf

International Monetary Fund (2014) *Global Prospects and Policy Challenges, Prepared for Meetings of G20 Finance Ministers and Central Bank Governors,* 22-23 February, Sydney, Australia, http://www.imf.org/external/np/g20/pdf/2013/022113.pdf

Irwin, N. (2013) *The Alchemists: Inside the Secret World of Central Bankers,* Business Plus, Headline Publishing Group, London.

Invest in France Agency (2013) *34 Sector-Based Initiatives for a French Industrial Renaissance,* http://www.invest-in-france.org/Medias/Publications/2222/34-sector-based-initiatives-for-a-french-industrial-renaissance-2013.pdf

Karanikolos, M., Mladovsky, P., Cylus, J., Thomson, S., Basu, S., Stuckler, D., Mackenbach, J. and McKee, M. (2013) Financial Crisis, austerity, and health in Europe, *The Lancet,* Vol. 381, 13 April, 1323-1331.

Katz, B. (2014) *The Hidden Line in Obama's Budget and What it Means for Cities and Metro Areas,* 7 March, Brookings Institution, Washington DC, http://www.brookings.edu/blogs/the-avenue/posts/2014/03/07-obama-budget-cities-katz

Keightley, M. (2013) *An Analysis of Where American Companies Report Profits: Indications of Profit Shifting,* Congressional Research Service, January, Washington DC, https://www.fas.org/sgp/crs/misc/R42927.pdf

Kennedy, G. and McIndoe-Calder, T. (2012) *The Irish Mortgage Market: Stylised Facts, Negative Equity and Arrears,* Central Bank of Ireland Quarterly Bulletin 01 January, http://www.centralbank.ie/publications/documents/the%20irish%20mortgage%20market%20stylised%20facts,%20negative%20equity%20and%20arrears.pdf

King, L. Kitson, M., Konzelmann, S. and Wilkinson, F. (2012) Making the same mistake again – or is this time different? *Cambridge Journal of Economics,* 36, 1-15.

Kinsella, S. (2012) Is Ireland really the role model for austerity? *Cambridge Journal of Economics,* 36, 223-235.

Krugman, P. (2013a) *End This Depression Now!* Norton & Company, New York.

Krugman, P. (2013b) How the Case for Austerity Has Crumbled, *The New York Review of Books,* 6 June, http://www.nybooks.com/articles/archives/2013/jun/06/how-case-austerity-has-crumbled/?pagination=false

Laeven, L. and Valencia, F. (2012) *Systemic Banking Crises Database: An Update,* IMF Working Paper WP/12/163, Washington DC, http://www.imf.org/external/pubs/ft/wp/2012/wp12163.pdf

Lafrance, X. and Sears, A. (2013) Campus fightbacks in the age of austerity: Learning from Quebec students, *Socialist Project E-Bulletin* No. 771, 9 February, http://www.socialistproject.ca/bullet/771.php

Lamarca, M.G. (2013a) Resisting evictions Spanish style, *New Internationalist,* April, http://newint.org/features/2013/04/01/sparks-from-the-spanish-crucible/

Lamarca, M.G. (2013b) Stopping evictions in Spain, *Polis,* January, http://www.thepolisblog.org/2013/01/stopping-evictions-in-spain.html

Lansley, S. and Reed, H. (2013) *How boost the wage share,* TUC Touchstone pamphlet No. 13, London.

Lawless, M., McCann, F. and Calder, T.M. (2012) *SMEs in Ireland: Stylised facts from the real economy and credit market,* Central Bank of Ireland, http://www.centralbank.ie/stability/Documents/SME%20Conference/Session%201/Paper%202/Paper.pdf

Levenson, D. and Istrate, E. (2011) *Access for Value: Financing Transportation Through Land Value Capture,* Metropolitan Policy Program, Brookings Institution, Washington DC, http://www.brookings.edu/~/media/research/files/papers/2011/4/28%20transportation%20funding%20levinson%20istrate/0428_transportation_funding_levinson_istrate.pdf

Levenson, Z. (2011) *Occupying Education: the student fight against austerity in California,* NACLA Report on the Americas, 44-6, November-December, 25-27.

Local Government Association (2013) *Local Authority Bonds: A local government collective agency,* London,
http://www.local.gov.uk/c/document_library/get_file?uuid=14a95f1c-287d-4d5d-a5c2-bc518144dace&groupId=10180

LocalGov (2013) *Bristol unveils first council-owned wind farm,* 4 October,
http://www.localgov.co.uk/Bristol-unveils-first-council-owned-wind-farm/28880

Long, C. (2013a) The real history of public pensions in bankruptcy, Muniland, *Reuters,* 8 August,
http://blogs.reuters.com/muniland/2013/08/08/the-real-history-of-public-pensions-in-bankruptcy/

Long, C. (2013b) Inflationumberitis, Muniland, *Reuters,* 26 July,
http://blogs.reuters.com/muniland/2013/07/26/inflationumberitis/

Long, C. (2013c) Mapping the pension blues, Muniland, *Reuters,* 26 November,
http://blogs.reuters.com/muniland/2013/11/26/mapping-the-pension-blues/

Long, C. (2014) Deep in the public pension weeds, Muniland, *Reuters,* 11 March,
http://blogs.reuters.com/muniland/2014/03/11/deep-in-the-public-pension-weeds/

Luce, S. (2012) What we can learn from Wisconsin? Chapter in Yates, M.D. Wisconsin *Uprising: Labor Fights Back,* Monthly Review Press, New York.

McCartin, J.A. (2013) Public Sector Unionism Under Assault: How to Combat the Scapegoating of Organised Labor. *New Labor Forum,* 22(3) 54-62.

MacInnes, T., Aldridge, H., Bushe, S., Kenway, P. and Tinson, A. (2013) *Monitoring Poverty and Social Exclusion 2013,* Joseph Rowntree Foundation and New Policy Institute,
http://www.jrf.org.uk/sites/files/jrf/MPSE2013.pdf

Maher, K. (2013) Worker Centers Offer a Backdoor Approach to Union Organizing, *Wall Street Journal,* 24 June,
http://online.wsj.com/article/SB10001424127887324144304578622050818960988.html

Marcos, J. (2014) Madrid abruptly cancels plans to outsource management at public hospitals, 27 January, *El Pais* http://elpais.com/elpais/2014/01/27/inenglish/1390844787_448815.html

Marti, J.B. (2012) Rearticulating the movement post-15M in Spain, *Open Democracy,* 8 October,
http://www.opendemocracy.net/jordi-bonet-marti/rearticulating-movement-post-15m-in-spain

Martin, B. and Rowthorn, R. (2012) *Is the British economy supply constrained II? A renewed critique of productivity pessimism,* Centre for Business Research, University of Cambridge, May,
http://www.cbr.cam.ac.uk/pdf/BM_Report3.pdf

Mather, S. (2013) Colombia Anti-Free Trade Strike brings gains for left, 25 September, *Counterpunch,*
http://www.counterpunch.org/2013/09/25/colombia-anti-free-trade-strike-brings-gains-for-left/

Mazzucato, M. (2013) *The Entrepreneurial State: Dubunking Public v Private,* Anthem Press, London.

Miller, M. (2011) *The Plague of the Nonprofits,* Shelterforce, February, http://www.shelterforce.org/article/2113/the_plague_of_the_nonprofits1

Mishel, L. and Bivens, J. (2011) *Occupy Wall Streeters are Right About Skewed Economic Rewards in the United States,* Economic Policy Institute, Briefing Paper No. 331, http://s1.epi.org/files/2011/BriefingPaper331.pdf

Mishel, L. (2012) *The Wedges between productivity and median compensation growth,* Issue Brief 330, 26 April, Economic Policy Institute, Washington DC, http://www.epi.org/files/2012/ib330-productivity-vs-compensation.2012-04-26-16:45:37.pdf

Molloy, C. (2013) *Victory for Lewisham hospital – but government's plan B threatens 100s more hospitals,* 29 October, http://www.opendemocracy.net/ournhs/caroline-molloy/victory-for-lewisham-hospital-but-governments-plan-b-threatens-100s-more-hosp

Moody's Investor Service (2012) *Spanish covered bonds issuers/ cover pools vulnerable to negative-equity credit risk,* 10 October, https://www.moodys.com/research/Moodys-Spanish-covered-bond-issuers-cover-pools-vulnerable-to-negative--PR_257281

Morris, J.A. (2012) Wisconsin's Painfully Moderate Labor Uprising, *Synthesis/Regeneration* 58, Spring, http://www.greens.org/s-r/58/58-14.html

Mosesdottir, L. (2013) The IMF´s Toxic Bail-out Of Greece And Iceland, *Social Europe Journal,* 11 July, http://www.social-europe.eu/2013/07/the-imf´s-toxic-bail-out-of-greece-and-iceland/

Murphy, R. (2012) *Closing the European Tax Gap, A report for Group of the Progressive Alliance of Socialists & Democrats in the European Parliament,* http://europeansforfinancialreform.org/en/system/files/3842_en_richard_murphy_eu_tax_gap_en_120229.pdf

Nation of Change (2013) *Portland's Austerity Resistance Movement Sparks Changes to City Budget,* 29 June, http://www.nationofchange.org/portland-s-austerity-resistance-movement-sparks-changes-city-budget-1372516783

National Audit Office (2013) *HM Treasury Resource Accounts 2012-13: The Comptroller and Auditor General's Report to the House of Commons,* July, London, http://www.nao.org.uk/wp-content/uploads/2013/07/HMT-Accounts-2012-13.pdf

National Coalition for Independent Action (2011) *Voluntary action under threat: what privatisation means for charities and community groups, May,* London, http://www.independentaction.net/2011/06/16/voluntary-action-under-threat-what-privatisation-means-for-charities-and-community-groups/

National Institute of Economic and Social Research (2013) *Macroeconomic impacts of infrastructure spending,* Report for the Trade Union Congress, April, http://www.tuc.org.uk/sites/default/files/tucfiles/infrastructure_spending.pdf

National Post (2013) *Opposition parties decry Canada Revenue Agency cuts after Conservatives vow to get tough on tax evasion,* 26 March, http://news.nationalpost.com/2013/03/26/opposition-parties-decry-canada-revenue-agency-cuts-after-conservatives-vow-to-get-tough-on-tax-evasion/

News of Iceland (2013) *Debt relief program in Iceland has been announced – 4.7% of GDP,* 1 December, Reykjavik

Nichols, J. (2012a) David Koch admits big spending to help Scott Walker bust 'union power', The Nation, 20 February, http://www.thenation.com/blog/166385/david-koch-admits-big-spending-help-scott-walker-bust-union-power

Nichols, J. (2012b) Recall Campaign against Scott Walker fails, *The Nation,* 5 June, http://www.thenation.com/blog/168242/recall-campaign-against-scott-walker-fails

Nichols, J. (2012c) *Uprising: How Wisconsin Renewed the Politics of Protest, from Madison to Wall Street,* Nation Books, New York.

Nkusu, M. (2013) *Boosting Competitiveness to Grow Out of Debt – Can Ireland Find a Way Back to Its Future?* IMF Working Paper WP/13/35, February, Washington DC, http://www.imf.org/external/pubs/ft/wp/2013/wp1335.pdf

Office for Budget Responsibility (2012) *Economic and Fiscal Outlook,* December, London. http://cdn.budgetresponsibility.independent.gov.uk/December-2012-Economic-and-fiscal-outlook 23423423.pdf

Office for National Statistics (2014) *Economic Review, February 2014,* 5 February, London, http://www.ons.gov.uk/ons/dcp171766_351740.pdf

Olney, P. (2013) AFL-CIO Follows Path of Least Resistance, *Labor Notes,* 22 October, http://www.labornotes.org/blogs/2013/10/viewpoint-afl-cio-follows-path-least-resistance

Onaran, O. and Galanis, G. (2012) *Is aggregate demand wage-led or profit-led? National and global effects,* Conditions of Work and Employment Series No. 40, International Labour Organisation, Geneva http://www.ilo.org/wcmsp5/groups/public/---ed_protect/---protrav/---travail/documents/publication/wcms_192121.pdf

Organisation for Economic Co-operation and Development (2012) *Employment Outlook 2012,* Paris, http://www.oecd.org/els/emp/EMO%202012%20Eng_Chapter%203.pdf

Organisation for Economic Co-operation and Development (2013a) *General government gross financial liabilities as a percentage of GDP,* Paris, http://www.oecd-ilibrary.org/economics/government-debt_gov-debt-table-en

Organisation for Economic Co-operation and Development (2013b) *Entrepreneurship at a Glance 2013,* Paris, http://dx.doi.org/10.1787/entrepreneur_aag-2013-4-en

Organisation for Economic Co-operation and Development (2013c) *Crisis squeezes income and puts pressure on inequality and poverty in the OECD,* Paris, http://www.oecd.org/els/soc/OECD2013-Inequality-and-Poverty-8p.pdf

Organisation for Economic Co-operation and Development (2013d) *OECD Secretary General Report to the G20 Leaders, St Petersburg,* 5-6 September, http://www.oecd.org/tax/SG-report-G20-Leaders-StPetersburg.pdf

Organisation for Economic Co-operation and Development (2013e) OECD Economic Outlook, Volume 2013 Issue 2, November, Paris, http://www.oecd-ilibrary.org/economics/oecd-economic-outlook-volume-2013-issue-2_eco_outlook-v2013-2-en

Ostry, J.,Berg, A. and Tsangarides, C. (2014) *Redistribution, Inequality and Growth,* Staff Discussion Note, International Monetary Fund, Washington DC, http://www.imf.org/external/pubs/ft/sdn/2014/sdn1402.pdf

Peck, J. (2014) Pushing Austerity: state failure, municipal bankruptcy, and the crisis of fiscal federalism in the United States, *Cambridge Journal of Regions, Economy and Society*

Peltier, J., Dahl, A. and Mulhern, F. (2009) *The Relationship between Employee Satisfaction and Hospital Patient Experiences,* University of Wisconsin and Northwestern University, Forum for People Performance, Management and Measurement,
http://www.info-now.com/typo3conf/ext/p2wlib/pi1/press2web/html/userimg/FORUM/Hospital%20Study%20-Relationship%20Btwn%20Emp.%20Satisfaction%20and%20Pt.%20Experiences.pdf

Pew Charitable Trusts (2013) *America's Bid Cities in Volatile Times,* November,
http://www.pewstates.org/uploadedFiles/PCS_Assets/2013/America's-Big-Cities-in-Volatile-Times.pdf

Pianta, M. (2013) *An Industrial Policy for Europe,* paper at European Association for Evolutionary Political Economy 2013 Conference, 7-9 November, Paris,
http://www.eaepeparis2013.com/papers/Full_Paper_mario-Pianta.pdf

Pivetti, M. (2013) On the Gloomy European Project: An Introduction, *Contributions to Political Economy,* 32, 1-10.

Pollin, R. (2012a) US government deficits and debt amid the great recession: what the evidence shows, *Cambridge Journal of Economics,* 36, 161–187.

Pollin, R. (2012b) Public policy, community ownership and clean energy, *Cambridge Journal of Regions, Economy and Society,* 2012, 5, 339–356.

Porter, E. (2013) Americanised Labor Policy is Spreading in Europe, *New York Times,* 3 December,
http://www.nytimes.com/2013/12/04/business/economy/the-americanization-of-european-labor-policy.html

PropertyWire (2013) *Negative equity figures decreasing in the US housing market,* 2 April,
http://www.propertywire.com/news/north-america/us-property-negative-equity-201304027617.html

PressTV (2013) *Portuguese wage major strike against austerity measures,* 27 June,
http://www.presstv.com/detail/2013/06/27/311063/portuguese-protest-austerity-measures/

PressTV (2013) *Madrid Celebrate Court's Decision to Block Health Privatization Plan,* 22 September, Madrid, http://www.presstv.ir/detail/2013/09/22/325460/madrid-celebrate-courts-decision-to-block-health- privatization-plan/

Principe, C. (2013) From mobilisation to resistance: Portugal's struggle against austerity, *International Socialism,* Issue 138, Spring, http://www.isj.org.uk/index.php4?id=884&issue=138

Principe, C. and Thun, A. (2013) What nest after Blockupy Frankfurt? *Socialist Project E-Bulletin* No. 838, 18 June, http://www.socialistproject.ca/bullet/838.php

Public Citizen (2013a) *The Trans-Atlantic 'Free Trade' Agreement (TAFTA),*
http://www.citizen.org/tafta

Public Citizen (2013b) *Salt Lake TPP Talks End with Growing Pressure to Announce 'Deal' at December TPP Ministerial, but No Resolution of Major Controversies,* November,
http://www.citizen.org/documents/update-on-salt-lake-tpp-talks.pdf

Quiggin, J. (2012) *Zombie Economics: How dead ideas still walk among us,* Princeton University Press.

Radice, H. (2012) 'Plan B': A new Alternative Economic Strategy? *Capital & Class,* 36: 207-213.

Radice, H. (2014) Enforcing austerity in Europe: the structural deficit as a policy target, *Journal of Contemporary European Studies* (Forthcoming).

Randle, A. and Kippin, H. (2014) *Managing Demand: Building Future Public Services,* Royal Society for the Arts, London,
http://www.thersa.org/__data/assets/pdf_file/0019/1540126/RSA_Managing-Demand_Revision4.pdf

RealtyTrac (2013) *Midyear 2013 U.S. Foreclosure Market Report,* 9 July,
http://www.realtytrac.com/content/foreclosure-market-report/midyear-2013-us-foreclosure-market-report-7794

Reed, H. and Mohun Himmelweit, J, (2012) *Where have all the Wages Gone?* TUC Touchstone Extra, London.

Reed, H. (2012) Plan B + 1, Compass and Friedrich Ebert Stiftung, London,
http://www.compassonline.org.uk/wp-content/uploads/2013/05/PlanB1.pdf

Rehmann, J. (2013) Occupy Wall Street and the Question of Hegemony: A Gramscian Analysis, *Socialism and Democracy,* Vol. 27, No. 1, 1-18.

Resolution Foundation (2013) *Closer to the Edge: Debt repayments in 2018 under different household income and borrowing cost scenarios,* December, London,
http://www.resolutionfoundation.org/wp-content/uploads/2014/08/Closer-to-the-Edge.pdf

Reuters (2013a) *Madrid's health workers strike over hospital privatisation,* 7 May,
http://www.reuters.com/article/2013/05/07/us-spain-austerity-health-idUSBRE9460PW20130507

Reuters (2013b) *Hollande turns to robots, driverless cars to revive French industry,* 12 September,
http://www.reuters.com/article/2013/09/12/us-france-industry-idUSBRE98B0HW20130912

Roberts, M. (2013) *Cash hoarding, profitability and debt,* 4 December,
http://thenextrecession.wordpress.com/2013/12/04/cash-hoarding-profitability-and-debt/

Rothschild, M. (2012) Accountability in Defeat in Wisconsin, *The Progressive.* 7 June,
http://www.progressive.org/accountability_in_defeat_in_wis.html

Sacramento Municipal Utility District (2013) *Annual report 2012,* Scaramento, California,
https://www.smud.org/en/about-smud/company-information/documents/2012-annual-report.pdf

Saez, E. (2013) *Striking it Richer: The evolution of Top Incomes in the United States* (Updated with 2012 preliminary estimates), University of California Berkeley,
http://elsa.berkeley.edu/%7Esaez/saez-UStopincomes-2012.pdf

Save Lewisham Hospital Campaign (2013) *Campaign's response to the Trust Special Administrator's draft report into the failure of South London Healthcare Trust (SLHT) as required under S18 of Health Care Act 2009.*

Sawyer, M. (2012) The tragedy of UK fiscal policy in the aftermath of the financial crisis, *Cambridge Journal of Economics,* 36, 205-221.

Schmitt, J. (2012) *Low-wage Lessons, Center for Economic and Policy Research,* January, Washington DC, http://www.cepr.net/documents/publications/low-wage-2012-01.pdf

Shepard, B.H. (2012) Labor and Occupy Wall Street: Common causes and uneasy alliances, *Working USA: The Journal of Labor and Society,* vol. 15, March, 121-134.

Siedle, E. (2013) Rhode Island Public Pension Reform: Wall Street's License to Steal, *Forbes,* 18 October, http://www.forbes.com/sites/edwardsiedle/2013/10/18/rhode-island-public-pension-reform-wall-streets-license-to-steal/

Silio, E. and Aunion, J. (2013) Cutbacks and PP government's reform plans fuel student's strike, *El Pais,* 24 October, http://elpais.com/elpais/2013/10/24/inenglish/1382635301_447233.html

Simpson, T. (2013) *We are all Greeks,* Spokesman Books, 11 November, http://spokesmanbooks.blogspot.co.uk/2013_11_01_archive.html

Sinclair, S. (2013) *Opening Remarks on Canada and the Trans- Pacific Partnership (TPP): Presentation to the House of Commons Standing Committee on International Trade,* 17 May, Ottawa, http://www.policyalternatives.ca/sites/default/files/uploads/publications/National%20Office/2013/06/Canada_and_the_Trans_Pacific_Partnership.pdf

Sirota, D. (2013) *The Plot Against Pensions, Institute for America's Future,* Washington DC, http://ourfuture.org/wp-content/uploads/2013/09/Plot-Against-Pensions-final.pdf

Smith, S. (2010) Nonprofits and Public Administration: Reconciling Performance Management and Citizen Engagement, *The American Review of Public Administration,* Vol. 40, No. 2, p129-152.

Stiglitz, J. (2013) *The Lessons of the North Atlantic Crisis for Economic Theory and Policy,* IMFdirect, 3 May, http://blog-imfdirect.imf.org/2013/05/03/the-lessons-of-the-north-atlantic-crisis-for-economic-theory-and-policy/

Stuckler, D, and Basu, S. (2013) *The Body Economic: Why Austerity Kills,* Allen Lane, London.

Slaughter, J. and Brenner, M. (2011) In the wake of Wisconsin, what next? in Yates, M.D., *Wisconsin Uprising: Labor Fights Back,* Monthly Review Press, New York.

Sloam, J. (2013) 'Voice and Equality': Young People's Politics in the European Union, *West European Politics,* 36:4, 836-858.

Snipes, R., Oswald, D., LaTour, M. and Amenakis, A. (2005) The effects of specific job satisfaction facets on customer perceptions of service quality: an employee-level analysis, *Journal of Business Research,* 58, 1330-1339.

Solidarity Against Austerity (2013) Austerity, Resistance and Results From Portland's Budget Process, 27 June, Portland.

Solty, I. (2012) Canada's Maple Spring? From the Quebec Student Strike to the Movement Against Neoliberalism, *Socialist Project E-Bulletin* No. 752, 31 December, http://www.socialistproject.ca/bullet/752.php

SOMO – Centre for Research on Multinational Corporations (2013) *Unanswered questions in the EC's roadmap,* http://www.somo.nl/dossiers-en/sectors/financial/eu-financial-reforms/newsletter-items/issue-20-october-november-2013/road-map-to-tackle-shadow-banking

Special Interest Group of Municipal Authorities (2013) *A Fair Future? The true impact of funding reductions on local government,* June, Barnsley, http://www.sigoma.gov.uk/Docs/sigomareports/A%20Fair%20Future%202013.pdf

Standard & Poor's (2013) *Economic Research: House Prices Are Still Falling In Most European Markets As The Recession Bites,* Ratings Direct, 25 July, http://www.standardandpoors.com/spf/upload/Ratings_EMEA/EuropeanhousingmarketsJuly2013.pdf

Stanford, J. (2013) *Good Time to Rethink Corporate Tax Cuts,* 14 November, The Progressive Economic Forum, http://www.progressive-economics.ca/2013/11/14/good-time-to-rethink-corporate-tax-cuts/

Stankova, M. (2013) *Bulgaria's on-going protests are driven by a society that refuses to tolerate further a political class that disregards democratic principles,* 20 July, http://blogs.lse.ac.uk/europpblog/2013/07/20/bulgaria-protest/

Stewart, J. (2014) *PwC/World Bank Report 'Paying Taxes 2014': An Assessment,* IIIS Discussion Paper No. 442, School of Business, Trinity College, Dublin, https://www.tcd.ie/iiis/documents/discussion/pdfs/iiisdp442.pdf

Stockhammer, E, (2013a) *Why have wage shares fallen? A panel analysis of the determinants of functional income distribution,* Conditions of Work and Employment Series No. 35, International Labour Organisation, Geneva, http://www.ilo.org/wcmsp5/groups/public/---ed_protect/---protrav/---travail/documents/publication/wcms_202352.pdf

Stockhammer, E. (2013b) Rising inequality as a cause of the present crisis, *Cambridge Journal of Economics,* forthcoming.

Stroud Against the Cuts (2012) *A landmark triumph for people power,* Press Release, 15 October, http://www.stroudagainstcuts.co.uk/fightback/healthcarecuts/38-healthcare/132-a-landmark-triumph-for-people-power.html

Sustainable Energy Authority of Ireland (2011) Biomass District Heating: A case study – The Mitchels Boherbee Regeneration Project.

Sutherland, J. (2013) *Spain's attacks are on fighting back,* Open Democracy, 17 May, http://www.opendemocracy.net/judith-sunderland/spain's-attacks-on-fighting-back

Syllas, C. (2013) *Greece: murder of anti-fascist prompts protest,* 19 September, http://www.indexoncensorship.org/2013/09/greece-murder-prompts-protests-politcal-moves-golden-dawn/

Taibbi, M. (2013) Looting the Pension Funds: All across America, Wall Street is grabbing money meant for public workers, *Rolling Stone,* 26 September, http://www.rollingstone.com/politics/news/looting-the-pension-funds-20130926

Tax Justice Network (2011) *The Cost of Tax Abuse: a briefing paper on the cost of tax evasion worldwide,* November, http://www.tackletaxhavens.com/Cost_of_Tax_Abuse_TJN_Research_23rd_Nov_2011.pdf

Tax Justice Network (2013a) *Press Release: response to OECD Action Plan on corporate tax avoidance, 19 July, http://blogs.euobserver.com/shaxson/2013/07/19/press-release-response-to-oecd-action-plan-on-corporate-tax-avoidance/*

*Tax Justice Network (2013b) Beyond BEPS: TJN briefing on the OECD's 'BEPS' project on corporate tax avoidance,* 17 July, http://www.taxjustice.net/cms/upload/pdf/TJN_Briefing_BEPS_final.pdf

The Equality Trust (2014) *The Cost of Inequality,* March, London, http://www.equalitytrust.org.uk/sites/default/files/The%20Cost%20of%20Inequality%20%20-%20full%20report.pdf

The Guardian (2013) *David Cameron: we need to do more with less ... permanently,* 11 November, http://www.theguardian.com/politics/2013/nov/11/david-cameron-policy-shift-leaner-efficient-state

The Huffington Post (2012) *Occupy Buffalo Helps Convince City Council To Divest From JPMorgan Chase After Trading Loss,* 31 May, http://www.huffingtonpost.com/2012/05/31/occupy-buffalo-jpmorgan-chase_n_1560579.html

Trade Union Congress (2013) *Four in five jobs created since June 2010 have been in low-paid industries,* Press Release 12 July, London, http://www.tuc.org.uk/economy/tuc-22364-f0.cfm

Van Treeck, T. and Sturn, S. (2012) *Income inequality as a cause of the Great Recession? A survey of current debates,* Conditions of Work and Employment Series No. 39, International Labour Organisation, Geneva, http://www.ilo.org/wcmsp5/groups/public/---ed_protect/---protrav/---travail/documents/publication/wcms_187497.pdf

Troost, A. and Hersel, P. (2012) *How a Socialisation of the German Banking System Might Look Like,* Rosa Luxemburg Stiftung, New York Office, October, http://www.rosalux-nyc.org/wp-content/files_mf/troosthersel_socializationofgermanbanking.pdf

Trottman, M (2013) AFL-CIO Members Back Link to Outside Groups, *Wall Street Journal,* 9 September, http://online.wsj.com/news/articles/SB10001424127887323864604579065491962718868

UNISON (2013a) *Rise in zero hour contracts shame councils and hit elderly and vulnerable,* 1 August, London, http://www.unison.org.uk/news/rise-in-zero-hours-contracts-shame-councils-and-hit-elderly-and-vulnerable

UNISON (2013b) *New research shows families thousands worse off,* Press Release, 20 June, London http://www.unison.org.uk/news/media-centre/new-research-shows-families-thousands-worse-off

United Nations Environment Programme Sustainable Energy Alliance (2009) *Why Clean Energy Public Investment Makes Economic Sense* – The Evidence Base, http://www.unep.org/pdf/dtie/WhyCleanEnergyPublicInvestment.pdf

University of California, Riverside (2011) Occupy Movement Spread to Small Towns and Cities in California, Newsroom, 15 December, http://newsroom.ucr.edu/2813

Van Biezen, I., Marir, P and Poguntke, T. (2012) Going, going, ... gone? The decline of party membership in contemporary Europe, *European Journal of Political Research* 51: 24–56.

Vandaele, K. (2013) Union responses to young workers since the Great Recession in Ireland, the Netherlands and Sweden: are youth structures reorienting the union agenda? *Transfer: European Review of Labour and Research,* 19(3) 381-397.

Varoufakis, Y., Holland, S. and Galbraith, J.K. (2013) *A Modest Proposal for Resolving the Eurozone Crisis,* Version 4.0, July, http://yanisvaroufakis.eu/2013/07/15/new-a-modest-proposal-for-resolving-the-euro-crisis-version-4-0-by-yanis-varoufakis-stuart-holland-and-james-k-galbraith/

Volintiru, C. (2012) *Romania's recent protests have become a social movement calling for the dignity of the people in the face of an unaccountable government,* 20 March, http://blogs.lse.ac.uk/europpblog/2012/03/20/romania-protests/

Wall Street Journal (2013a) *Canada Household Debt Sets New High,* 13 December, http://online.wsj.com/news/articles/SB10001424052702303932504579255992964972128

Wall Street Journal (2013b) *US corporate profits soar in 2012. Workers get little of it,* 28 March, http://blogs.marketwatch.com/thetell/2013/03/28/u-s-corporate-profits-soar-in-2012-workers-get-little-of-it/

Wall Street Journal (2013c) *More US Profits Parked Abroad, Saving on Taxes,* 10 March. http://online.wsj.com/article/SB10001424127887324034804578348131432634740.html

Wall Street Journal (2013d) *Volcker Rule Challenges Wall Street,* 10 December, http://online.wsj.com/news/articles/SB10001424052702303560204579249732841592834?mod=WSJEUROPE_hps_LEFTTopWhatNews

Wall Street Journal (2014a) *Detroit files debt cutting plan,* 21 February, http://online.wsj.com/news/articles/SB10001424052702303775504579396992180729508

Wall Street Journal (2014b) *Proliferation in Student Debt Driven By Weakest Borrowers, Fed Finds,* 18 February, http://online.wsj.com/news/articles/SB10001424052702303491404579391251354067462

Whitfield, D. (2001) *Public Services or Corporate Welfare: Rethinking the Nation State in the Global Economy,* Pluto Press, London.

Whitfield, D. (2006) *New Labour's Attack on Public Services: Modernisation by Marketisation,* Spokesman Books, Nottingham.

Whitfield, D. (2010) *Global Auction of Public Assets: Public sector alternatives to the infrastructure market and Public Private Partnerships,* Spokesman Books, Nottingham.

Whitfield, D (2012a) *In Place of Austerity: Reconstruction of the state, economy and public services,* Spokesman Books, Nottingham. http://www.spokesmanbooks.com/acatalog/Dexter_Whitfield.html#a601

Whitfield, D. (2012b) *The Mutation of Privatisation: A critical assessment of new community and individual rights,* European Services Strategy Unit Research Report No 5, July, http://www.european-services-strategy.org.uk/publications/essu-research-reports/the-mutation-of-privatisation-a-critical-asses/mutation-of-privatisation.pdf

Whitfield, D. (2012c) *PPP Wealth Machine: UK and Global trends in trading project ownership,* European Services Strategy Unit Research Report No. 6, http://www.european-services-strategy.org.uk/ppp-database/ppp-equity-database/ppp-equity-report-final-full.pdf

Whitfield, D. (2012d) Plan B and beyond, *Red Pepper,* February/March, http://www.redpepper.org.uk/plan-b-and-beyond/

Whitfield, D. (2013a) *Unmasking Austerity: Lessons for Australia,* Australian Workplace Innovation and Social Research Centre and European Services Strategy Unit, August, http://www.adelaide.edu.au/wiser/docs/WISeR_unmasking-austerity.pdf

Whitfield, D. (2013b) Should we turn the NHS into co-ops and mutuals, *Open Democracy,* 14 November,
http://www.opendemocracy.net/ournhs/dexter-whitfield/should-we-turn-nhs-into-co-ops-and-mutuals

Whitfield, D. (2014) *PPP Database: Strategic Partnerships 2012-2013,* European Services Strategy Unit, http://www.european-services-strategy.org.uk/ppp-database/ppp-partnership-database/ppp-strategic-partnerships-database-2012-2013.pdf

World Economy, Ecology and Development (2013) *Financial services in the planned EU-US trade agreement TTIP,* November, Berlin,
http://www2.weed-online.org/uploads/factsheet_financial_services_ttip.pdf

World Health Organisation, Regional Office for Europe (2013) Health, health systems and economic crisis in Europe: Impact and policy implications, Summary,
http://www.euro.who.int/__data/assets/pdf_file/0011/186932/Health-and-economic-crisis-in-Europe4.pdf

Wolf, M. (2013) How Austerity Has Failed, *New York Review of Books,* 11 July,
http://www.nybooks.com/articles/archives/2013/jul/11/how-austerity-has-failed/?pagination=false

Yates, M.D. and Chowdhury, F. (2012) Occupy Wall Street and the US Labor Movement, *Synthesis/Regeneration* 58, Spring, 16-20.

Yates, M.D. (2011) *Wisconsin Uprising: Labor Fights Back,* Monthly Review Press, New York.

Yates, M.D. (2013) The War on Public School Teachers, *Socialist Project E-Bulletin* No. 854, 22 July,
http://www.socialistproject.ca/bullet/854.php

Zandi, M. (2010) *Perspectives on the Economy, Moody's Analytics,* Testimony to House Budget Committee, 1 July, https://www.economy.com/mark-zandi/documents/Final-House-Budget-Committee-Perspectives-on-the-US-Economy-070110.pdf

Zettelmeyer, J., Triebesch, C. and Gulati, M. (2013) *The Greek Debt Restructuring: An Autopsy,* Working Paper 13-8, Peterson Institute for International Economics, August, Washington DC,
http://www.iie.com/publications/wp/wp13-8.pdf

Zhong, R. (2013) Andrew Haldane: The Banker Who Cried 'Simplicity', *Financial Times,* 20 December,
http://online.wsj.com/news/articles/SB10001424052702304858104579263190940438738?mod=djemITPE_h